. . . And the wine is bottled poetry . . .
Robert Louis Stevenson

Other Books in the Show Me Missouri Series:

99 Fun Things To Do in Columbia and Boone County

A to Z Missouri: The Dictionary of Missouri Place Names

Complete Katy Trail Guidebook

Daytrip Missouri

Forgotten Missourians Who Made History

The River Revisited—Reflections in the Wake of Lewis and Clark

River Rat's Guide to Missouri River History and Folklore

River Valley Companion—A Nature Guide

Wit & Wisdom of Missouri's Country Editors

Exploring Missouri WINE Country

Wine is light, held together by water.
— Galileo

Brett Dufur

Pebble Publishing
Columbia, Missouri

Project support by Pebble Publishing staff:
Addie & R.C. Adams, Brian Beatte, Tawnee Brown, Brett Dufur, Daisy Dufur,
Mark Flakne, Pippa Letsky, Scott Angus, Jeff Lehman and Heather Starek

ISBN 0-9646625-6-6 14.95

Cover photograph by Brett Dufur. Overlook of Hermann taken from Hermann Hill
Vineyard and Inn. Aerial photograph on back cover by Sandy Watts.

Pebble Publishing, P.O. Box 431, Columbia, MO 65205-0431
Phone: 1 (800) 576-7322 • Fax: (573) 698-3108
E-Mail: Pebble@showmestate.com
Online: Katytrail.showmestate.com & Trailsidebooks.com

Printed by Ovid Bell Press, Fulton, Missouri, USA

To Tawnee with love.

Acknowledgments

Many thanks go to all of the vintners who made exploring Missouri wine country such an enriching experience. Murli Dharmadhikari, enology advisor, and Sanliang Gu, the viticulture advisor, at the Department of Fruit Science Research Campus at Southwest Missouri State University contributed vital information, as did Denise Kottwitz and Jim Anderson of the Missouri Grape and Wine Program. I am also gratefully indebted to the following people for generously sharing their time and expertise: Archie Beatte, Mary Mueller of Röbller Winery; Jim Ashby and Lucinda Huskey of Stone Hill Winery; Greg Stricker, past president of the Missouri Winemaking Society; Dr. Bourgeois, Kristein King, Cory Bomgaars and Chad Thomas of Les Bourgeois Winery & Vineyards; Department of Natural Resources' state historian Jim Denny and site administrator for Deutschheim Historical Site Dr. Erin Renn; Christopher Roussin director at Cavern Springs Winery; Lucy Valbuena, Amy Scheidegger and Jessica Faerber of Hermannhof Winery; editors Sandy Watts and Nancy Fagerness of the *Missouri Wine Country Journal;* and Julaine Cabot of the Hermann Visitors Association. Thanks also go to Ken Luebbering, co-author of *German Settlement in Missouri,* and Robert Scheef, author of *Vintage Missouri.* Special thanks also go to friends, family and everyone at Pebble Publishing who went the extra mile on this project: R.C. Adams, Brian Beatte, Hope Wagner, Tawnee Brown, Alan Westenbroek, Neal Dufur, Kathy Dufur, Mark Flakne, Heather Starek, Scott Angus, Jeff Lehman, Pippa Letsky and, of course, Addie, Beckley, Matisse, Magellan, Crispy and Daisy.

CONTENTS

Preface 8
Introduction 10
Getting Started 12
Commonly Asked Wine Country Questions 14
History 16
How to Use This Book 23
Wine Regions:

AUGUSTA REGION

Marthasville Vineyards, Marthasville 28
Blumenhof Vineyards & Winery, Dutzow 31
Augusta Winery, Augusta 35
Montelle Winery, Augusta 37
Mount Pleasant Wine Company, Augusta 39
Sugar Creek Winery, Defiance 43
Cavern Springs Winery, St. Charles 48
Winery of the Little Hills, St. Charles 50

HERMANN REGION

Adam Puchta Winery, Hermann 60
Hermannhof Winery, Hermann 63
Stone Hill Winery, Hermann 66
Bias Vineyards & Winery, Berger 73
Röbller Vineyard & Winery, New Haven 77

CENTRAL REGION

Les Bourgeois Winery & Vineyards, Rocheport 84
Buffalo Creek Vineyards & Winery, Stover 91

WESTERN REGION

Bristle Ridge Vineyards & Winery, Knob Knoster 100
Bynum Winery, Lone Jack 103
Pirtle's Weston Vineyards, Weston 107

CONTENTS

OZARK HIGHLANDS REGION

St. James Winery , St. James 114

Ferrigno Vineyards & Winery, St. James 117

Heinrichshaus Vineyard & Winery, St. James 119

Peaceful Bend Vineyards & Winery, Steelville 125

Reis Winery, Licking 130

OZARK MOUNTAINS REGION

Gloria Winery & Vineyard, Mountain Grove 135

Stone Hill Winery—Branson, Branson 139

SOUTHEAST REGION

Sainte Genevieve Winery, Ste. Genevieve 144

River Ridge Winery, Commerce 148

Special Sections:

The Best and the Biggest 150

Budding Wineries Ripe for Exploration 151

Wine Outlets 152

Grape Varieties 154

Making Wine 162

Tasting Wine 169

How to Store and Care For Wine 169

History of the Bottle 172

Starting a Vineyard 176

Edible Landscaping 181

Bibliography 182

Glossary 184

Index 188

Winery Quick Reference Guide 192

PREFACE

Curving Ozark roads have always lured me with promises of new discovery. They quietly await the inquisitive wanderer to seek them out, so they might impart the rich heritage of our state.

On some of these gorgeous backroads, atop bluffs and rolling hills, there are vintners blending an art and a craft into a lifestyle that many of us only dream about. Their profession combines a unique balance of agriculture and old world art, which often instills admiration from newcomers.

For many, curiosity about a wine and its inception lingers long after the glass is empty. The story of Missouri's winemaking is a rich one, and the saga continues today. So get out there and explore! This guidebook answers many wine questions for both beginners and pros. In addition to highlighting Missouri's wine regions and every winery found within them, this book includes nearby services and history, introduces newcomers to tasting and appreciating wine, explains the grape varieties grown and serves as an introduction to the families and faces of Missouri's burgeoning wine industry.

There are currently 30 wineries around the state. In 1995, sales of Missouri wine reached a post-Prohibition high of more than 300,000 gallons. So about one bottle in 20 sold within the state is Missouri-made. This definitely marks a peak in today's wine revolution. But underlying today's success stories is a prolific past. Before Prohibition in 1920, Missouri was home to no less than 65 wineries, and was producing ten times as much wine. In 1904 alone, Missouri wineries produced a record 3 million gallons of wine. In fact, 100 years ago, Missouri was the second largest wine-producing state in the nation—behind only New York.

But as much as this book is about today's wine revolution, it's also a book about the immigrants and the rich countryside that supported the initial evolution of such a fruitful wine country. As you drive these hills and walk into today's wineries, remember that by 1860, more than half of Missouri's foreign-born residents were German. The rich German heritage of our wine regions has left a legacy in winemaking as well as an imprint on our architecture and day-to-day life.

It would be hard to imagine a modern-day Missouri without German influence. German immigrants gave us foods such as the jelly doughnut, apple butter, potato salad, hamburgers and sauerkraut. Even kindergarten is a German concept. A family-oriented Christmas, complete with gifts, sweets and a decorated evergreen tree was introduced to a great extent by these early German settlers. Even "Silent Night," the most popular Christmas carol in America, comes from a German-speaking country. These early immigrants also brought with them an architectural style that is still well preserved today in towns throughout Missouri, such as Hermann and Westphalia. Many of their festivals, such as Maifest and Oktoberfest, continue today.

Before that first drop of wine touches your tongue, there are other senses waiting to be tantalized. A stroll through a vineyard hanging heavy with fruit, a bluff-top view of a mist-filled valley below, a gentle breeze enjoyed under a pergola of vines, a taste of a new wine and a walk through the damp coolness of a seasoned wine cellar, all await your exploration.

I hope this book will increase your appreciation of Missouri wine and the progressive winemaking taking place here. The laborious behind-the-scenes work that goes into each bottle is remarkable. Twelve-hour days in sweltering heat. Back-breaking labor. Patience. Ah, the glorious life of winemaking. Yet life among the vines and the art of winemaking have long held a romantic mystique. From the early Greek's homage to a god of wine, alternately called Dionysus and Bacchus, to more modern studies by George Washington and Thomas Jefferson, the process evokes an image of old world art and celebrates virtues such as patience, hard work and family togetherness.

Nowhere else do these virtues and old world influence match up so perfectly with back roads and quiet bluff-top settings than in Missouri wine country. The wineries and vineyards throughout the state have become havens for day-trippers, explorers and a growing class of wine drinkers. For me, the beautiful part of exploring Missouri wine country is that there is no strip mall of wineries. To really enjoy these wineries, adventure is in order. As Mark Twain once said, "There's more to traveling than arriving."

Read on to discover the tumultuous evolution of Missouri's wine industry, which has grown immensely in the past 10 years. The vintners themselves have even been surprised by the explosive growth. This growth is due to several factors including the increasing quality of Missouri wines, state assistance, better marketing, a maturing industry, a new generation of well-educated winemakers, healthier lifestyles, the increasing consumer demand for locally brewed spirits and the publication of fine guidebooks (if I do say so myself).

So read on . . . a journey of discovery awaits!

Brett Dufur
Pebble Publishing
Rocheport, Missouri

INTRODUCTION

As I gaze out at the rolling hills and white church steeples of Hermann from my second-story office window at Stone Hill Winery, I'm reminded of the importance of wine to this community and the entire state of Missouri. Once home to 65 wineries, Hermann flourished for 70 years as the nation's second largest wine-producing region. As it was in the glory years before Prohibition, wine is once again an integral part of the economic base of Hermann and many other towns in Missouri.

I'm proud to have grown up with the Missouri grape and wine industry, and I am particularly ecstatic to witness the recent explosion in the popularity of our state's great wines. I can remember presenting Missouri wines at tastings not so long ago . . . watching as countless patrons marched right past my table in search of California or imported wines. I practically had to beg people to stop and give our wine a chance. But our wines weren't in vogue, and admittedly, many of

---

During the past five years, the ratio of medals awarded to the 30 Missouri wineries has actually been higher than those awarded to the more than 750 California wineries . . .

---

them weren't as good as they are now. Whether or not the people had ever tasted Missouri wines, however, there was a natural bias against them. The glamour and Hollywood-style promotion of the California wineries overshadowed ours, and I often wondered if Missouri wines would ever be tasted objectively and given the credit they were due.

Then, Missouri vintners began entering wines and winning medals in major national and international competitions. The nice thing about wine competitions is that they are conducted blind. In other words, none of the prestigious judges can see the labels. So, some of the same stuffy wine writers who may have cracked jokes about "non-California" or "other" wines were unwittingly awarding medals to Missouri wines! As a matter of fact, during the past five years, the ratio of medals awarded to the 30 Missouri wineries has actually been higher than those awarded to the more than 750 California wineries.

With the awards came a considerable amount of press coverage, and now Missouri vintners can't seem to make enough wines to satisfy their enthusiastic followers. Today, wine tastings are a pleasure. People flock to the Missouri wine tables to taste the new vintages, and chat excitedly to their friends about their last adventure in Missouri wine country. And that's another reason for the success of Missouri wines—our vineyards and wineries are nestled in some of the most picturesque settings in the country. It's a necessity in Missouri to situate our vineyards on high bluffs overlooking river valleys so that our tender vines can be protected from harsh winter blasts and spring frosts. Our beautiful Ozark plateaus and river hills, coupled with the historic winery buildings, provide a breathtaking scenery that delights flatlanders and city folk. Once visitors take a tour through a series of 150-year-old vaulted stone cellars and spend the night in a nearby historic bed & breakfast, they are hooked forever and bring friends and family back again and again.

Indeed, the future for the Missouri grape and wine industry is bright. All of the elements for a world-class wine region are in place. Our long growing season produces grapes of superior quality. Our vintners have committed themselves to excellence by purchasing state-of-the-art equipment and sending their sons and daughters to the finest enology schools—and all of this with a history of once having produced more than 40 percent of the nation's wine!

I urge you to explore Missouri wine country. Meet the Italians in the St. James–Rosati area, the Germans in Hermann and Augusta, and the French in Ste. Genevieve. Taste the wines and the foods indigenous to each area and enjoy the good old-fashioned Missouri hospitality that abounds in each region. You will have a great time, and I'll bet we'll see you more than once. *Gemütlichkeit!* (Good times with good friends.)

> *Jim Ashby*
> Director of Marketing — Stone Hill Winery
> Hermann, Missouri

GETTING STARTED

Start . . .

. . . whenever you can
. . . wherever you are

There's never a better time than right now to visit a Missouri winery. A winery tour at any time of the year will likely give you the opportunity to catch some aspect of the winemaking process in action.

Like other forms of agriculture, the cycle of "growing wine" follows the seasons. The vintner's work alternates between growing, processing and marketing the wine. Steps include winter pruning of the vines, caring for the spring's new shoots, tending the vines all summer long, managing the autumn crush and finally, guiding the wine through maturity. In this way, winemaking is a craft, demanding continuous labor and care by the artist, from conception through execution.

The seasons change, the vines grow and the grapes are transformed into wine. So many variables are part of the process, yet one aspect remains unchanged—constant contact with the public. Every day the winemaker pours samples of recent releases and receives immediate evaluations for his effort. Missouri winemakers enjoy hosting visitors, whether introducing them to the world of wine or revealing insights about their craft.

TOUR TIPS

Missouri's wine country can be enjoyed in many ways

Touring Wine Country by Car

If you are looking for a great back-road adventure, visit a Missouri winery. If you live near St. Louis, a tour on Sunday afternoon can take you to many of Missouri's wineries along Highway 94 and Highway 100. If you live in Kansas City, there are five wineries within a two-hour drive.

Use the map at the beginning of each region to help you plan your next excursion. No matter where you live in Missouri, there will almost always be a winery near you or one "just far enough away" for that perfect daytrip or bed & breakfast weekend.

Drink Responsibly!

Don't drink and drive. Part of the fun of any journey is getting to and from your destination safely. A designated driver is always the way to go.

Touring Wine Country by Bicycle

Touring France's wine country by bike is a classic wine-connoisseur's dream. Before you learn to say "No" to *"Parlez-vous français?"* . . . a similar experience can be had much closer to home. I recently guided a 5-day bicycle trip along the 200-mile Katy Trail, which passes through Missouri's Augusta, or Weinstrasse, region. I was leading a group of wine lovers from Chicago, so we toured many of the wineries along the way. The previous year, they had toured France's wine country by bike and said this trip exceeded their experience abroad. They found great wine, cozy bed & breakfasts and fine dining here—and they were more than happy to pay $10–25 for a bottle of wine instead of $100 a bottle in France. *Vive le Misuri!*

For more complete Katy Trail information, refer to my book, *The Complete Katy Trail Guidebook* or check out the *Interactive Katy Trail* on the Internet at: katytrail.showmestate.com.

Touring Wine Country by Train

Amtrak runs daily between St. Louis and Kansas City. With stops in Hermann, Washington, Jefferson City, Sedalia, Warrensburg, Lee's Summit and Independence, you can spend the day enjoying Hermann, for example, or design your own wine country weekend. A round-trip ticket was $52 as of June 1997. Call Amtrak at 1 (800) USA-RAIL for more information.

Touring Wine Country by Boat

Several Missouri wineries are also accessible by boat. Both the Missouri and the Meramec Rivers provide convenient access to wine country, and Buffalo Creek Vineyards and Winery is completing a tasting room on the Lake of the Ozarks.

From Washington, heading west, a quick jaunt up the Missouri River to New Haven (along with an adventurous spirit and a friendly person willing to give you a lift) will get you to Röbller Vineyard and Winery. Mary Mueller at Röbllers said Nick down at the Penelope Boat Dock and Fuel Stop will often take boaters up to the winery, located about a mile away. However, don't show up on a sunny weekend and expect him to always leave his post.

A boat trip further west takes you by some of the most impressive bluffs along the Missouri River. Head to Rocheport's Les Bourgeois Winery & Vineyards. Their bistro overlooks both the river and the Katy Trail. The bistro isn't directly accessible from the river. However, go up Moniteau Creek, located on the north side of town, and there's a landing on the right (before the Katy Trail bridge).

In the Ozarks, Peaceful Bend Vineyards and Winery has a set-up smack-dab on the Meramec River. They even offer wine in plastic bottles for boaters. A short hike takes you through their forested property and up to the main tasting room.

COMMONLY ASKED
WINE COUNTRY QUESTIONS

How do I use this book?
We've divided the book into seven regions. Find a specific winery using the table of contents, index, page headers or the listing of wineries inside the back cover.

How many wineries are there in Missouri?
There are currently 30 wineries operating in the state, but several new ones are planning to open soon. Call the Grape and Wine Program at 1 (800) 392-WINE or see the listing in the back of the book for more details.

What should I expect when I visit?
Expect a totally new experience. Missouri wines consistently win national and international awards. Their wines are unique to Missouri, however, so don't be surprised when you don't find your favorite California-style Zinfandel.

What's the best time of day to visit a winery?
Most wineries close at dusk, so get there early. I've shown up at dusk and found tasting rooms already closed.

What's the price range of Missouri wines?
Most Missouri wines retail from $7 to $25 a bottle. Ice wines and other specialty wines are often bottled in 375 ml "half bottles" to keep the prices below $25. Most wineries give quantity discounts when you purchase four or more bottles. Prices are not listed in this book since offerings and prices change frequently.

Should we bring our kids?
Definitely! All wineries sell juices and pop to quench their thirst. They make a special effort to accommodate the entire family—so bring the kids!

What's the best winery to visit?
My advice is—visit as many as you can and decide for yourself. From one-man operations to multimillion-dollar ventures, every winery offers something worth exploring.

What's the best month to see grapes being harvested?
The picking season begins in August and ends in October. At smaller wineries and vineyards you may even get a chance to help.

How about a wine country weekend. Any suggestions?
I've included bed & breakfast listings, other services and histories for each town to help you plan your perfect wine country weekend.

How far in advance do I need to make reservations at a B & B?
To insure a successful wine country weekend, book your reservations well in advance. During Oktoberfest in Hermann, most B & Bs are booked a year in advance, but this is certainly not the norm.

How is wine made?
We've included a special section that takes you from the vine to the wine. Refer to the back of this book for answers.

What makes a wine a Missouri wine?
Missouri wine must be produced from at least 85 percent Missouri-grown grapes. When harvests are below average, this percentage can be reduced to 75 percent.

What's an ice wine?
Ice wines are super-sweet dessert wines, made from grapes with a high sugar content. These grapes are harvested in late fall, after cold weather has increased the grape's sweetness. Authentic ice wine is made from grapes that have been left to freeze on the vines.

I need help! I just bought your book and I'm desperate to impress my girlfriend this weekend.
No sweat. We've included *The Basics of Tasting Wine*, on page 169 just for you.

Are the wineries wheelchair accessible?
While some wineries have paved ramps, it's best to call in advance.

GRAPE FACT

Augusta:
America's First Approved Viticultural Area

Four of the approved 129 viticultural areas in the United States are in Missouri. They are the Hermann, Augusta, Ozark Mountains and Ozark Highlands viticultural regions. Each federally-recognized area has defined borders and specific qualities of climate, soil, elevation and geographic features which distinguish it from other areas. In 1980, Augusta was the first region in the country to be approved by the Bureau of Alcohol, Tobacco and Firearms.

A rendering of the joyous moment Tyrker found grapes growing in Vinland.

THE EARLY HISTORY OF THE AMERICAN GRAPEVINE

Explorers named North America "Vinland"

The written history of North American vineyards begins with the legend of Leif Ericsson's voyage to an unknown land in 1000 A.D. One version of this much-disputed account tells how Tyrker, a German on Ericsson's ship, discovered a plant with wine berries. Impressed by this discovery, Ericsson named the new land "Vinland" and returned home with samples.

Many historians believe that Tyrker probably found wild cranberries. They cite evidence that Ericsson landed on the northern coast of present-day Newfoundland, where the climate is too cold for grapevines. Nevertheless, future Europeans would come to marvel at the abundance and tenacity of North America's native grapevines. In fact, there are more native grape species in North America than on any other continent.

Fertile soils and an amicable growing climate set the stage for the development of a North American wine industry. Later, even George Washington and Thomas Jefferson grew vines for winemaking and were early supporters of the idea of turning America into a world-class wine producer.

THE HISTORY OF MISSOURI WINE

Immigration surges with Missouri's entry into statehood

When Missouri achieved statehood in 1821, tens of thousands of immigrants came looking for a better life. Many were escaping political, religious and economic oppression in Europe. Missouri's abundant and virtually untapped resources attracted large numbers of immigrants from Germany, France, Switzerland, Austria and eventually Italy. The rich soils, expansive waterway connections, timber and abundant game made Missouri a veritable Eden for the poor and landless.

German Author Favors Settlement in Missouri

In 1824, Gottfried Duden, an optimistic traveler from Germany, arrived on Missouri soil. He believed that many of Germany's woes resulted from overpopulation and poverty. Thinking emigration was the solution to these problems, Duden and his friend Louis Eversmann had set sail for America to study the possibilities of German settlement in the United States.

A view of Hermann in the 1800s.

Arriving in St. Louis, Duden and Eversmann found Nathan Boone, son of Daniel Boone and surveyor of government lands. Boone led them on a tour of the Missouri River valley. Leaving the area several days later, the German duo lost their way and headed west instead of east. Soon they found the home of Jacob Haun, of Pennsylvania German descent. Haun talked them into purchasing adjoining tracts of land, near present-day Dutzow, and offered to shelter and feed them until they could establish their own farms. Duden agreed. For almost three years he lived in a cabin near Lake Creek, recording the weather, growing conditions and daily doings on his farm. In 1829 Duden published his findings back in Germany and it soon became a best-seller. The next excerpt is from his initial observations.

"I do not conceal the fact from you that the entire life of the inhabitants of these regions seemed to me like a dream at first," Duden wrote. "Even now, after I have had three months to examine conditions more closely, it seems to me almost a fantasy when I consider what nature offers man here." He went on to describe "acorns . . . as big as hen's eggs and wild grapevines . . . heavy with sweet fruit."

The Editor's Introduction to the English translation of Duden's book called the *Report of a Journey to the Western States of North America:*

> *. . . a masterpiece of promotional literature. Duden's adroit pen wove reality with poetry, experience with dreams, and contrasted the freedom of the forests and democratic institutions in America with the social narrowness and political confusion of Germany. He glorified the routine of pioneer existence, praised Missouri's favorable geographical location, and emphasized its mild and healthy climate. . . . So overwhelmed with what he saw and experienced, Duden feared Germans would not believe him: "It appears," he wrote, "too strange, too fabulous."*

To struggling—even starving—Germans back home, these words offered an almost irresistible allure of freedom and plenty. Feeling the oppression back home, the promotional writings of many Germans, including Duden's glowing account, inspired thousands of Germans to emigrate to the "New Rhineland."

GRAPE FACT

The Isabella

The first Native American grape on record to be made into wine in Missouri was the Isabella. This grape is believed to have its "roots" in South Carolina. Hermann farmers planted Isabella, hoping to capitalize on the tenacity of the stock. Unfortunately, Isabella didn't produce the results they desired, so it was abandoned for varieties like Catawba and Norton.

Hermann vineyards, circa 1900.

Old World Winemaking Reaches Missouri

As German settlers pushed westward, many carried carefully-wrapped clippings from their old world vineyards. Many of the groups traveled down the Ohio River from Cincinnati, to the Mississippi and up to the mouth of the Missouri River at St. Louis, right in the footsteps of Gottfried Duden.

Moving to a new land caused a deep yearning to preserve their heritage. In 1836, the German Settlement Society was intent on establishing a new "Fatherland" in America. They selected some land on the south bank of the Missouri River, west of St. Louis, and founded Hermann. The original town was laid out with some plots originally sold as wine plots, beginning in the 1840s. Though their settlement met with many hardships and the soil on the hills nearby wasn't appropriate for many forms of agriculture, by 1846 they had produced their first wine from locally cultivated grapes. In 1848, the town's wineries produced 1,000 gallons. By 1855, 500 acres of vineyard were in production and wine was being shipped to St. Louis and beyond.

But wine in Hermann didn't become a huge money-maker until after the Civil War. It was in 1866 that Missouri surpassed Ohio as the second largest wine growing state in the Union. By 1869, 42 percent of America's wine was produced in Missouri.

Railroads further boosted the growth of the Missouri wine industry, but the completion of the first transcontinental route in 1869 also made it possible to market California wines in the eastern United States. These California wines became very popular because they were made from grapes more familiar to the Europeans. However, Missouri's wine production continued to flourish. It remained second only to California until Prohibition.

By the turn of the century, Stone Hill Winery, which the German immigrant Michael Poeschel began building in 1847, was the third largest winery in the world (second largest in the U.S.), producing more than a million gallons of wine a year. Its wines, such as Hermannsberger, Starkenberger and Black Pearl, won eight gold medals at world fairs between 1873 and 1904.

Italian immigrants also played an important role in Missouri's first vineyards. Many Italians had ventured to Arkansas with the intention of working as sharecroppers on the cotton plantations. Some members ended up in the Ozark Highlands of Missouri near St. James. It was here that they began to cultivate vineyards keeping with the traditions of their homeland.

Missouri Vines Save
European Vineyards from Parasites

As trellises spread across the landscape, Missouri viticulture soon raised another flag of worldwide acclaim. In 1867, an insidious louse began a relentless assault on vineyards throughout France. The parasite had come from America and found the French roots particularly appealing—pushing the French wine industry to the brink of ruin.

Fortunately, Missouri's first entomologist (bug scientist) Charles V. Riley made an important discovery. In 1871, at the invitation of the French government, Riley inspected France's ailing grape crop. He diagnosed the problem as an infestation of *phylloxera,* an American plant louse. He found that some Native American rootstocks were immune to the advances of the dreaded louse. By grafting French vines onto them, healthy grapes could be produced. Millions of cuttings of Missouri rootstock were shipped to save the French wine industry from disaster. Statues in Montpelier, France, commemorate this rescue.

Although this next fact has nothing to do with wine, its worth mentioning and highlights Riley's flair for innovative problem solving. During a severe grasshopper plague in western Missouri in 1875, Riley suggested that rather than go hungry, farmers should eat the insects. To introduce people to the delicacy he offered his friends fried grasshoppers. Once he even served a four-course meal consisting of grasshopper soup, baked grasshoppers, grasshopper cakes, grasshoppers with honey and just plain grasshoppers.

Prohibition—The Dark Years

Before Prohibition, there were wineries in 48 Missouri counties. Bluffton, Boonville, Cape Girardeau, Hannibal, Owensville, and Stanton were just a few of the many towns that boasted wineries. Long before anyone had ever heard of Harry Truman, Independence was known for its wine production by companies such as Shaffer's Winery and Lohse's Native Wine Garden.

In fact, Missouri's Weinstrasse region grew to include more than 100 wineries before coming to an abrupt halt in 1920 with the addition of the 18th amendment to the Constitution—Prohibition—which prohibited the manufacture and sale of alcohol in the United States. This amendment dealt a fatal blow to Missouri's wine industry. Vines were burned or abandoned and winemaking equipment was destroyed. Many families lost their livelihood. At Stone Hill Winery, Ottmar Stark ordered all of his vineyards destroyed, virtually ruining the local economy.

In fact, the survival of many historic buildings in Hermann is largely attributed to the economic downturn caused by Prohibition. Instead of destroying older homes and building new ones, the old buildings were continually lived in and kept up, which allows us to appreciate early German construction even today.

The only Missouri winery to survive this dry period was the St. Stanislaus Novitiate, located in St. Louis, where Jesuits continued to produce sacramental wine. Following repeal of the act in 1934, Missouri's wine industry was nothing but a memory. High liquor taxes and license fees discouraged the industry's rebirth. A few dozen wineries did reopen, but much of Missouri remained legally dry, and there was little demand for anything other than sweet, dessert-style wines.

GRAPE FACT

Cass County Carry

One Missouri woman's painful marriage to a heavy drinker fueled the drive to Prohibition. When her marriage was over, Cass County native Carry Nation spent the rest of her life in a crusade against alcohol. She wrote editorials, gave lectures and formed temperance groups—but she really put the cork on her place in history by smashing up saloons with a hatchet. She usually went to the bar mirror first, which left her in hatchet-range of all the bottles and decanters.

Missouri's Wine Industry Revival

In the last 30 years, a handful of visionary vintners have labored to restore many of Missouri's vineyards and wineries to their pre-Prohibition levels of excellence. It's fitting that this rebirth started in Hermann, when Jim and Betty Held switched from raising mushrooms in Stone Hill's cellars to making wine again.

The state government has helped promote the rebirth of Missouri viticulture. In 1980 the Missouri Wine Advisory Board was formed and a state enologist was hired. Since that time a new tax on wine sales has helped generate funds for a state-run Grape and Wine Program. A portion of this money supports a research program at Southwest Missouri State University's Fruit Experiment Station. Scientists there are studying varieties of grapes from around the world in hopes of identifying those varieties best suited for Missouri viticulture.

In 1980, Augusta became the first official viticultural region in the country, approved by the Bureau of Alcohol, Tobacco and Firearms. Since then, Hermann, the Ozark Highlands and the Ozark Mountain region have also made this list.

Today, more than 30 vineyards and wineries are pressing grapes for wine every fall. Gallonage of wine produced in Missouri has nearly doubled since 1991. A new generation of Missouri vintners, many schooled in California, are working with proven grape varieties and methods, producing increasingly complex and sophisticated wines.

Many wineries, old and new, are winning medals at home and abroad. Much to the pleasure of wine lovers in Missouri and elsewhere, the state's wine industry is thriving once again.

WELCOME TO
MISSOURI WINE COUNTRY

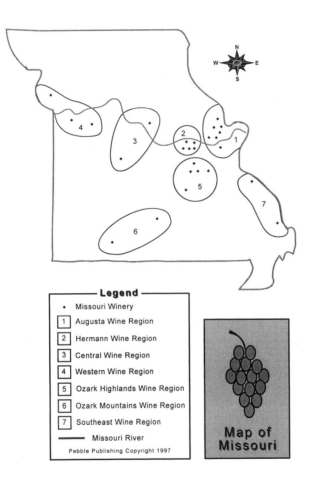

Legend
- ◆ Missouri Winery
- [1] Augusta Wine Region
- [2] Hermann Wine Region
- [3] Central Wine Region
- [4] Western Wine Region
- [5] Ozark Highlands Wine Region
- [6] Ozark Mountains Wine Region
- [7] Southeast Wine Region
- —— Missouri River

Pebble Publishing Copyright 1997

Map of Missouri

HOW TO USE THIS BOOK

This book is divided into seven geographic regions: Augusta, Hermann, Central, Western, Ozark Highlands, Ozark Mountains and the Southeast. To locate a specific town or winery, please refer to the table of contents, index or the back cover.

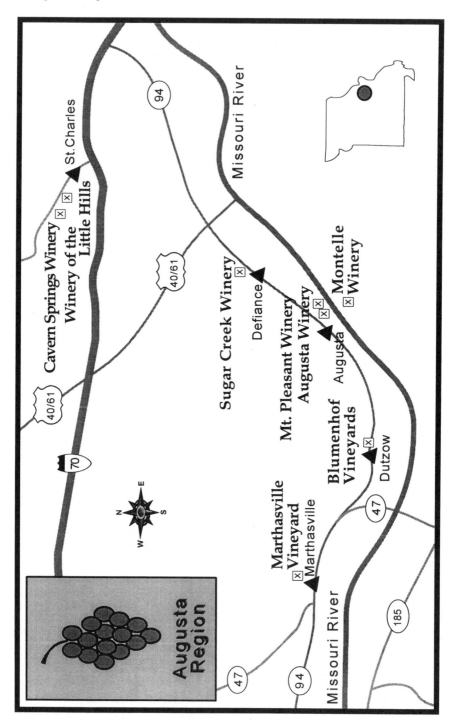

AUGUSTA REGION

Most of the wineries in this region lie along the *Weinstrasse* (German for wine road). This corridor runs along the Missouri River, following Highway 94. The wineries here are popular destinations for St. Louisans eager to spend a weekend in the countryside, head out on a short daytrip or simply find a quiet place to watch another day come to a close.

The wineries are located within an hour of each other, making a day tour of all of them possible.

If you are looking for a day's worth of adventure that will take you to a wide range of Missouri wineries, the Augusta Wine Region is a fine place to start.

EXPLORING MARTHASVILLE
Marthasville Vineyards

B & Bs • Bikes • Eats • Gas • Lodging • Parking • Post Office • Restrooms
Shelter with Picnic Tables • Shuttle Service • Water
Marthasville Chamber of Commerce: (314) 433-5242

Pioneer settlement in the Marthasville area began as fur traders and trappers arrived in the La Charrette area in the late 1700s. Daniel Boone's arrival in 1799 signified the continued approach of American colonization. When Lewis and Clark passed this way on their way west in 1804, this was the last pioneer settlement they passed in Missouri.

If you enjoy history, Marthasville will not disappoint. The settlement at the site of present-day Marthasville was named for Dr. John Young's wife, Martha, in 1817. In 1835, Augustus Grabs built what are now the Grabs House Museum and Rusche Park. Prearranged tours are available. Downtown, the old buildings still have the original metal facades (storefronts) and stories of ghosts in the old MK&T boardinghouse abound.

Daniel Boone and his wife, Rebecca, were originally buried nearby on a tree-covered knoll overlooking Toque Creek. Their remains were subsequently moved to Frankfort, Kentucky, in the 1840s, with the consent of the Boone family. The monument at their original burial site stands as a tribute to the old Quaker. Ask most locals, however, and you'll get a different story. Locals attest that the wrong body was pulled from its resting place and taken to Kentucky.

The arrival of the Katy Trail in 1990 has helped revive Marthasville as much as the MK&T Railroad did almost a century earlier. Since the Katy Trail's completion in 1996, Marthasville residents have hosted many folks traveling long distances to ride and experience the Katy. Visitors have come from places as diverse as Austria, England, the Virgin Islands, Germany, Brazil, Australia and many regions of the United States.

If you'd like to take a leisurely pedal along the Katy Trail in Marthasville, Scenic Cycles is truly a biker's oasis. Owners Terry and Cathy Turman rent bikes, kid carts and quadricycles, which are four-wheeled bikes that seat two and pedal and steer easily. Cathy says the quadricycles are the perfect solution for those wanting to take their elderly or physically-challenged friends out into the trail's outdoor bliss.

Bed & Breakfasts

Concord Hill B & B	Gramma's House B & B
(314) 932-4228	(314) 433-2675

Bike Rental
Scenic Cycles
203 Depot Street • (314) 433-2909

Daniel Boone was originally buried near present-day Marthasville.

How to Get to the Daniel Boone Monument: This monument is on . . . you guessed it . . . Daniel Boone Monument Road, which is a blacktop road 1.5 miles east of Marthasville. Once you're back on Highway 47, keep an eye out for the signs, and a white house and tan shed off to the north. Take this road north (towards the bluff). The road Ts within sight of the Katy Trail. Go left and follow the road 1.2 miles and the monument is on the right. The monument is tucked in between cedar trees and early grave markers.

Daniel Boone in Missouri

Not far from Daniel Boone's burial site, outside of Marthasville, lies his home near Defiance. The house is only a few miles from the Katy Trail. It is furnished as it was when Daniel died on September 26, 1820. Boone's home can be visited by calling (314) 987-2251. Or if you're within 25 miles in any direction, you can't miss the bright orange signs that lead you right to it. Gates close at 5 p.m. sharp.

Boone came to Missouri in 1799, after spending most of his life in North Carolina, Virginia, Kentucky and West Virginia. Spain still controlled the Missouri country then and Boone was one of the first Americans to respond to the Spanish government's invitation to settle the territory. He was appointed chief officer to the Femme Osage area in 1800. His duties included justice of the peace and militia commandant. He also divided up land for incoming pioneers. It was from his home in Defiance that Boone wrote the following passage:

> *I am hire With my hands full of Bisness and No athoraty,*
> *and if I am Not indulged in What I Do for the best it Is Not*
> *worth my While to put my Self to all this trubel . . .*

The prominent lettering atop the silo in Marthasville signals your arrival.

MARTHASVILLE VINEYARDS

304 Depot Street, Marthasville, MO 63357
(314) 433-5859
Hours of Operation:
Monday through Friday 11 a.m. to 5 p.m.
Saturday 10 a.m. to 5:30 p.m. & Sunday 11 a.m. to 5:30 p.m.
During winter, weekends only

HOW TO GET THERE: From I-70, take Route 47 south to Marthasville.

Two weeks after this winery opened its doors in 1993, the worst flooding in a century closed them again. Water four feet deep filled the winery, located a stone's throw from the Katy Trail and the Missouri River.

Owner Joe Meiners reopened the winery in 1994. In 1996 Meiners changed the name from Charrette Creek Winery to Marthasville Vineyards, to tie the winery closer to the historic town.

Marthasville Vineyards is a great place to take a break on the large shaded patio after hiking or biking on the Katy Trail. The tasting rooms are the highlight of this stop, since though there are no vineyards present. Inside the Scarlet Room, you will find the actual wraparound bar used on the set of *Gone with the Wind*, and later in *Meet Me in St. Louis*. The mayor of St. Louis bought the bar in 1977 and it moved out to Marthasville in 1994 from a club in the city.

Their wine labels are also unlike any other in the state. They were created by famous wildlife artist Ray Mangin, who lives in New Mexico. Two percent of all proceeds from the sale of Marthasville Vineyards wine are donated to the National Wildlife Coalition in Martha's Vineyard, Massachusetts.

MARTHASVILLE WINE LIST

Current Offerings:
BOTTLE NOSE DOLPHIN: A dry white wine made from Seyval grapes—crisp and light similar to Sauvignon.
GORILLA MIST: A delicate semi-dry white wine made from Vidal grapes. Forward fruit flavors—similar to Chardonnay.
HARBOR SEAL WHITE: A sweet, white wine—premium aperitif.
KILLER WHALE RED: A full-bodied dry red wine, a classic premium wine made from Norton grapes—similar to Merlot.
SCARLET RED MACAW: A dry red wine with a light body and fruity aroma—similar to Cabernet Sauvignon.
SWEET MANATEE RED: A sweet table wine with a distinct fruit flavor.
SWEET SWIFT FOX: A fruity sweet blush wine similar to White Zinfandel.

Two percent of all proceeds from the sale of Marthasville Vineyards wine are donated to the National Wildlife Coalition in Martha's Vineyard, Massachusetts.

EXPLORING DUTZOW
Blumenhof Vineyards & Winery

Bikes • Eats • Parking • Post Office • Restrooms
Call the Marthasville Chamber of Commerce
For more information: (314) 433-5242

Missouri's German heritage first took root in Missouri around present-day Dutzow. In the 1820s, Gottfried Duden established a farm on nearby Lake Creek and sent enthusiastic accounts of his experiences (compiled into a book, *Report on a Journey to the Western States of North America*) back to Germany. In 1832, Baron Wilhelm von Bock founded the town of Dutzow making it the first German settlement in Missouri.

Many early intellectuals' romantic notions of living on the frontier quickly dissolved, too daunted by their lack of farming skills to stay in the wilderness. Many soon returned to city life in St. Louis or headed back to Germany.

A second wave of German settlers, however—knowing full well the challenges that lay ahead—soon arrived in the area. They were led by Friedrich Muench and Paul Follenius. Muench planted several vineyards around Dutzow and became well known for his expertise in the cultivation of grapes. He also went on to become a Missouri senator. A stone barn with Muench's name in the keystone still stands in Dutzow.

By 1839, Jesuit priests were also coming regularly to Dutzow. A parish was soon established and the first Saint Vincent de Paul Church was built in 1842.

The railroad followed in the 1890s and the town prospered. Like most river-town sagas, however, the railroad era soon gave way to interstate commerce. Dutzow remains a small, vibrant town that is a favorite destination for daytrippers out of St. Louis on a weekend drive, for antique hunters and for bikers who come here to ride the Katy Trail.

Eats
Dutzow Deli
(314) 433-5118

Bike Rental
Katy Bike Rental, Inc.
(314) 433-KATY

"This is the only winery we go to," says Dawn Matschiner, from St. Louis, enjoying a sunny Monday afternoon with her friends.

BLUMENHOF VINEYARDS & WINERY

Highway 94, P.O. Box 30, Dutzow, MO 63342
(314) 433-2245
Hours of Operation:
Monday through Saturday 10:30 a.m. to 5:30 p.m.
Sunday noon to 5:30 p.m.

HOW TO GET THERE: Less than an hour by car from the St. Louis area, Blumenhof Winery is located in Dutzow on Highway 94, just 8 miles west of Augusta. Blumenhof is also a convenient stop for bicyclists on the Katy Trail, since the trail passes right in front of the winery.

This winery offers a relaxing atmosphere in German decor. Blumenhof's name, which translates from German as "Court of Flowers," honors the Blumenberg's ancestral farm located in the foothills of the Harz Mountain in northwest Germany.

The 1997 growing season marked the 10th anniversary for this winery, owned by the father and son team of Jim and Mark Blumenberg. Mark planted the first cuttings here in 1979. Since then, the Blumenhof Winery has established itself as an award-winning winery despite being one of the youngest in the area. More

The Blumenhof's tasting room and deck.

than 80 wine bottles now line the tasting room, dangling medals and acclaims from California to Indiana.

Blumenhof's wines have won medals at the Missouri State Fair, from the *Dallas Morning News*, the Florida State Fair, the International Eastern and the California National Orange Show wine competitions. These appreciated wines are produced almost exclusively from grapes grown in the Blumenhof vineyards.

Chief vintner Mark Blumenberg currently has about 14 acres in production, but several more acres of young plants are well on their way towards maturity. The Blumenhof Winery places special emphasis on the production of dry varietals but also has a variety of wines to suit a wide range of preferences.

Open 361 days a year, the winery hosts a series of outdoor concerts in the spring and fall. Tours are given by appointment and complimentary tastings are offered in their tasting room.

BLUMENHOF WINE LIST

Current Offerings:
CAYUGA WHITE: Similar to the Cayuga of the wineries of New York where it originated. Cayuga White is a grape that performs well in the Blumenhof vineyards, producing light and flowery Germanic wine.

CHAMBOURCIN: A medium-bodied varietal wine with firm berry fruit tones complemented by toasty oak.

CHARDONEL: This dry white wine is made from the Chaumette Vineyards in Ste. Genevieve County. This offering is fermented in French Oak, aged for 10 months and bottled unfiltered.

CHARRETTE WHITE: White wine that is a blend of several white varieties, primarily Seyval and Vidal Blanc.

GOLDBLUMEN: Made from the Vidal Blanc grapes picked in November, this is a flavorful after-dinner wine. This wine won a silver medal at the 1996 Missouri Wine Competition.

KATY'S BLUSH: Made in the style of a White Zinfandel.

MISSOURI WEINLAND: Vidal Blanc made in a semi-dry style, with floral aromas and a bit of spiciness. Gold medal winner at the 1996 Missouri Wine Competition.

NOUVEAU: This fruity red is made from 100 percent Chambourcin grape.

RAYON D'OR: Made from the Rayon d'Or grape. An appley, semi-dry wine.

SEYVAL: A crisp, light varietal wine with a bouquet of cut hay and spearmint.

VIGNOLES: With scents of pears, pineapples and spring flowers and a beguiling flavor of rich, ripe, succulent fruit, this wine was a gold medal winner at the 1996 Missouri Wine Competition.

VINTAGE RESERVE VIDAL BLANC: 100 percent Vidal Blanc fermented and aged in French oak barrels. A rich, full-bodied wine with an elegant balance of fruit and oak.

EXPLORING AUGUSTA

Augusta Winery, Montelle Winery, Mount Pleasant Wine Company

B & Bs • Bikes • Craft shops • Eats • Gas • Lodging
Parking • Post Office • Restrooms
Augusta Visitors Association: (314) 228-4005

Leonard Harold, one of Daniel Boone's followers to St. Charles, founded this town in 1836. The site was chosen for its excellent river landing. Before Harold's survey, it was a campsite for French fur traders, and a spot along one of the more popular Native American trails.

By the time of its incorporation in 1855, the town was known as Mount Pleasant. The town changed its name to Augusta when it applied for a post office and learned that the name Mount Pleasant was already in use.

Augusta was also a popular riverboat landing known as Augusta Bend. In 1872, flooding of the Missouri River caused the river to fill in its main channel, changing its course and cutting Augusta off from the river. Fortunately for the town, the railroad was soon to follow. The new land between the town and the river also provided great commercial potential.

Located atop a gently rolling landscape, the vineyards surrounding Augusta have been recognized for their ability to produce superior wine grapes since the 1800s. Augusta actually became America's first recognized viticultural area, or official wine district, in 1980, because of the distinctive soil type and the length of growing season within this 15-square-mile region.

As other towns have gone by the wayside, Augusta, with its 300 residents, is still a thriving small town. Much of the tourist interest, which was spurred by the revival of the vineyards in the late 1960s, has blossomed into the many home-based businesses you see today. According to the locals, if a flag is flying near the door, you can be sure the business is open.

Bed & Breakfasts

Ashley's Rose Restaurant and B & B
(314) 482-4108

Lindenhof Country Inn
(314) 228-4617

H.S. Clay House
(314) 482-4004

Augusta Wine Country Inn
(314) 482-4307

Bike Rental
Touring Cyclist
(314) 482-4038

The Augusta Winery is located in the middle of town. There are no vineyards present, but its tasting room and wine garden please the palate.

AUGUSTA WINERY

P.O. Box 8, Augusta, MO 63332
(314) 228-4301
Hours of Operation
Monday through Saturday 10 a.m. to 6 p.m.
Sunday noon to 6 p.m.

HOW TO GET THERE: From St. Louis, take Highway 40 west to Highway 94. Travel south on 94 for 18 miles to Augusta. From Kansas City, take I-70 east to Highway 47. Travel south on 47 to Highway 94. Take 94 north to Augusta.

A drive of less than an hour from St. Louis, through the scenic Missouri River valley, brings you to Augusta Winery. This winery is located in the center of town on the corner of High and Jackson Street.

The winery features wines ranging from dry dinner wines to sweet dessert wines. Owner/vintner Tony Kooyumjian and his staff craft all of Augusta Winery's wines from locally grown grapes. They produce up to 20,000 gallons each year, and their friendly sales staff assist you with the many varieties in the tasting room. Step outside and enjoy the terrace with a chilled bottle of wine and a picnic lunch. Locally produced cheese and sausage are also available.

AUGUSTA WINE LIST

Current Offerings:

BLACKBERRY WINE: Semi-sweet, flavorful fruit wine with deep color.

CHAMBOURCIN: A dry full-bodied red with rich, complex fruit flavors.

CYNTHIANA: Dry, full-bodied red with intense flavors. Aged in oak.

RESERVE RED: A fruity semi-dry red, light-bodied with a soft finish. This wine has received a gold medal "Best of Class" award and bronze medal.

RESERVE WHITE: A dry white with a floral bouquet, rich fruit flavors and a lingering toasty finish. This wine was the winner of 2 silver medals.

RIVER VALLEY BLUSH: A fruity, salmon colored, semi-dry blush.

RIVER VALLEY RED: A sweet dessert wine with a cherry color, fresh berry flavor and aroma and a long finish. This wine has received one bronze medal.

RIVER VALLEY WHITE: A sweet dessert wine with a rich fruit bouquet and flavor and a long finish. This wine is the winner of 2 silver medals.

SEYVAL BLANC: A semi-dry white with crisp acidity, intense fruit flavors and a lingering finish. A winner of numerous awards and medals.

VIDAL BLANC: A spicy dry white with a toasty floral bouquet, crisp acidity and a rich finish. This wine has received 2 silver medals and 3 bronze medals.

VIGNOLES: A semi-sweet white with a bouquet of strawberry and melon and a fresh crisp fruit body with a hint of sweetness.

VINTAGE PORT: Deep burgundy, rich and full-bodied.

Bob Slifer stores his barrels vertically using a block system he first saw in California.

MONTELLE WINERY

P.O. Box 147, Augusta, MO 63332

(314) 228-4464

Hours of Operation:

Monday through Saturday 10 a.m. to 5:30 p.m.

Sundays noon to 5:30 p.m.

HOW TO GET THERE: From St. Louis take Highway 40-64. Take Highway 94 south 15 miles to the winery. Watch for their signs.

The Montelle Winery sits high above the Missouri River valley. Visitors can enjoy a great view of Augusta, the river, and the vineyards from the tasting room or the picnic area. Montelle Winery is a destination that brings you through the heart of the Augusta Region. The winding highway twists and turns, carrying you past picturesque hillsides, meadows and farmland. A daytrip here provides many opportunities to explore.

Robert Slifer developed an appreciation for wine in Belgium in the 1960s, while he was working there as a chemical engineer. When he and his wife, Judy, returned stateside they started looking into Missouri's wine-producing possibilities, and met Clayton Byers who was creating wines in the French style they had come to enjoy in Europe. "One thing led to another," Slifer says, and soon he had retired from engineering to enter the wine business with Byers.

Slifer and his wife have now operated Montelle Winery for 17 years. Using grapes grown on the 25-acre vineyard, they produce about 8,000 cases or 100,000 bottles each year. "We're learning all the time," Slifer says. "You never know everything about wine—there's always something else to learn."

Be sure and check out the new Montelle wine labels by Missouri's renowned steamboat artist, Gary Lucy. The label features the painting *The Bright Star*, c. 1873, plying the treacherous Missouri River from Washington to Augusta.

MONTELLE WINE LIST
Current Offerings:

CABERNET SAUVIGNON

DeCHAUNAC

FIESTA

GLACIER WHITE

HOLIDAY WAY (Saint Wenceslaus)

JULIET

MISS KITTY ROUGE

NOBLE VIGNOLES

NORTON

OSAGE BLUSH

RESERVE DUMONT

RIVER COUNTRY WHITE

ROSE GOLD

SEYVAL

SOIGNÉ

SPARKLING GOLD

STONE HOUSE RED

VIDAL

MONTELLE
1996 Semi-Dry
River Country White

The road into Augusta is flanked by rows of healthy vines.

MOUNT PLEASANT
WINE COMPANY

5634 High Street, Augusta, MO 63332
(314) 482-4419 or 1 (800) 467-9463
Hours of Operation:
Monday through Saturday 10 a.m. to 5:30 p.m.
Sunday 11 a.m. to 6 p.m.

HOW TO GET THERE: From St. Louis, take Highway 40 west to Highway 94. Travel south on 94 for 18 miles to Augusta. From Kansas City, take I-70 east to Highway 47. Travel south on 47 to Highway 94. Take 94 north to Augusta.

George Muench and his brother Fredrick began planting the Mount Pleasant vineyards in the late 1800s. The brothers had emigrated from Germany with the idea of establishing a classic, old world winery in the heart of Missouri's Rhineland. The buildings were built using Augusta limestone and handmade bricks manufactured on the property. Their wines were receiving international acclaim when Prohibition put an end to their endeavor. During this dark period, all activity at the winery stopped and vineyards were destroyed.

Some 40 years later, the vineyards were replanted and the Mount Pleasant winery was resurrected. Today, the winery is once again producing exceptional

Visitors from
Germany . . .
ferrets . . .
You never know who
or what you're going
to run into.

wines from grapes grown in the 60-acre vineyard. Tim Peters and Mark Baehmann are the resident vintners and Phillip Dressel and his children Charles and Anne are the owners. Each year they produce about 40,000 gallons of wine, including ports and champagnes. Many varieties have returned Mount Pleasant to the winner's platform at international wine competitions. Mount Pleasant was also recently voted Missouri's favorite winery by a poll of St. Louisans in the *Riverfront Times*.

Visits to Mount Pleasant often begin in the tasting room. After making a selection, their spacious and inviting decks and gazebos offer a front-row view of the sun setting across the Missouri River valley.

The winery also hosts live music, barbecues, private parties and receptions year-round. The terrace rooms hold up to 250 people and are the perfect place for special gatherings.

MOUNT PLEASANT WINE LIST

Current Offerings:

AUGUSTA VILLAGE: Medium-bodied red aged in Missouri oak.

BARREL-FERMENTED SEYVAL: Full-flavored, creamy white with oak aromas.

BRUT IMPERIAL: Dry, sparkling wine with crisp flavors and light salmon color.

CHARDONNAY RESERVE: Full-bodied white flavored of butter, apple and oak.

COUNTRYSIDE BLUSH: Promotes powerful citrus flavors.

CYNTHIANA: Dry, full-bodied red with berry and oak flavors. Long finish.

FIFTEEN BARREL TAWNY PORT: Bright, pale amber. Medium-bodied with full acidity and medium sweetness. Flavors of golden raisins, toffee and pralines.

GENESIS CHAMPAGNE: Yeasty and toasty. Crisp acidity and balanced fruit tones.

HARVEST SELECT RED: Sweet red with heavy fruit tones.

HARVEST SELECT WHITE: Sweet white wine made from a blend of French hybrids. Fruity nose and clean, fruity flavor.

HIGHLAND RED: Semi-dry red with berry tones.

HILLSIDE RESERVE: Oak-aged, medium-bodied with fruity aroma.

ICEWINE 1995: Flavors of apricots, honey and caramel.

JRL'S BARREL SELECT PORT: Rated one of best ports in the country. Rich, full-bodied.

MISSOURI RHINELAND: Premium white wine blend. Semi-dry white. Balanced acidity and sweetness.

PEARL OF OMAN: From muscat grapes. Sparkling wine with foxy aroma and fruit flavors.

PINOT NOIR: Medium-bodied and flavored of tannins and spice.

RAYON D'OR: Well-balanced, off-dry white.

SEYVAL BLANC: Dry white reminiscent of Sauvignon Blanc.

TEN BUCKS: Sparkling wine with sweet flavors.

VIDAL BLANC: A "Missouri Chardonnay." Soft, buttery, oak flavor.

EXPLORING DEFIANCE

Sugar Creek Winery

Bikes • Eats • Lodging • Parking • Post Office • Restrooms
Call the Trading Company of Defiance for Katy Trail information: (314) 987-2765

Early settlers in the Defiance area were of English descent, from Virginia and Kentucky. In 1798, David Darst settled in the area and Thomas and Phoebe Parsons purchased the claim of Joe Haynes (land grant number 14) in 1839. The Parsons family owned most of the land where the town was built. He built a brick house on the bluff, which is now the Parsons House B & B. James Craig, aware of the significance of the railroad to small towns, led a crusade to build a depot and a farm-to-market road (now Defiance Road). The town was then named Defiance because it had lured the railroad away from Matson in 1893.

The Schiermeier store here represents the interdependence between farmers and the railroad. The store has two opposite-facing fronts. This boomtown phenomenon allowed one front to face the railroad, while the other front faced the farmers and local agriculture.

Bed & Breakfasts

Das Gast Haus Nadler
(314) 987-2200

Parson's House B & B
(314) 798-2222

Bike Rentals

Katy Bike Rental
2998 South Highway 94
(314) 987-2673

Seasons & Memories
2886 South Highway 94
(314) 987-2203

A river bottom view along Highway 94, near Dutzow.

SUGAR CREEK WINERY

125 Boone Country Lane, Defiance, MO 63341
(314) 987-2400
Hours of Operation:
Monday through Saturday 10 a.m. to 6 p.m., Sunday noon to 6 p.m.
Closed Thanksgiving, Christmas and New Year's.
(Winter hours vary, so please call for information.)

HOW TO GET THERE: The winery is located 12 miles southwest of Highway 40-61 on Highway 94. Follow 94 west of Defiance to a steep hillside that rises from the Katy Trail and overlooks the broad Missouri River valley. Watch for the signs.

T he Sugar Creek Winery is located along the Katy Trail in a turn-of-the-century Victorian home that embodies the romantic atmosphere of the wine industry.

Ken and Becky Miller make their wines from American and French hybrid grapes, grown in their vineyards surrounding the winery. Inside the house you will find the Sugar Creek tasting room housed in an intimate parlor, wrapped in fantastic stained glass, which also has many wine-related souvenirs for sale.

The Millers' winery was formerly Boone Country Winery, but they renamed it when they purchased the property in August of 1994. They made the move from Kirkwood (a suburb of St. Louis) to Defiance and brought the name of their former neighborhood with them—Sugar Creek. A colorful mural on the side of a shed, an expansive view and abundant outdoor seating just steps from the vineyard make this a great place to sip a new wine and relax with a friend. Next to their winery is an ornate gazebo where live music is often played and barbecues are held on the last Sunday of each month from April through October.

SUGAR CREEK WINE LIST

Current Offerings:

BIRDLEGS BLUSH: This Chambourcin and Chenin Blanc blend has fresh citrus tones with a lively finish.

BLACKBERRY THICKET: Classic fruit wine.

BOONE COUNTY WHITE: A crisp, fragrant Riesling-style wine.

LA RUSTIC RED: Four grape varieties blended together offer a sweet wine ripe with cherry and wild berry flavors.

LA RUSTICA WHITE: A balanced blend of Seyval and Vidal grapes—slightly sweet and fruity start with a dry finish.

PEACH HOLLOW: Fruit wine with a light and sweet texture.

RASPBERRY PATCH: Fruit wine with strong raspberry tones.

SEYVAL BLANC: A crisp, fruity dry white wine aged in French oak.

SIGNATURE PORT: After-dinner dessert wine.

SUNSET RED: This smooth, semi-dry red has spicy berry flavors.

VIDAL BLANC: A dry, light Chardonnay-style dinner wine aged in French oak.

EXPLORING ST. CHARLES

Cavern Springs Winery, Winery of the Little Hills

B & Bs • Bikes • Camping • Casino • Crafts • Eats • Gas • Hostel • Lodging
Microbrewery • Parking • Restrooms • RV hookups
Visitors Center: (314) 946-7776 or 1 (800) 366-2427

A visit to downtown St. Charles, which was once the capital of Missouri, feels like walking into a historical photo. The cobblestone of Main Street works its rhythm beneath your feet as you stroll past antique shops and ice-cream parlors along this friendly ten-block corridor into the past.

Pass the afternoon in the shade, walk the Katy Trail or join in a game of frisbee down by the river. The activity in St. Charles doesn't set with the sun. So if you're not in a hurry, you might try your luck on one of the riverboat casinos docked within walking distance of the Katy Trail or dine outside at one of the many tempting restaurants and cafés nearby.

Founded as Les Petites Cotes (The Little Hills) by French Canadian fur trader Louis Blanchette in 1769, this area became the headquarters for the fur-trading industry along the Missouri River. By 1791, the population had grown to 255 and the second Catholic church was dedicated to San Carlos Borromeo (1538–1584), archbishop of Milan and patron saint of Charles IV, king of Spain. On the day the church was dedicated, the town changed its name to San Carlos.

San Carlos was "Americanized" to St. Charles in 1804 during the formalization of the Louisiana Purchase. In subsequent years, St. Charles, like many other Missouri towns, was greatly affected by western expansion, German immigration, the 1849 California Gold Rush, and railroad and river trade.

Before Missouri was granted statehood in 1821, various locations had served as the government seat for territorial affairs. As statehood became a certainty, the permanent site of Jefferson City was chosen. But until the new Capitol could be constructed, nine cities vied for the honor of hosting the state's temporary seat of government. The citizens of St. Charles furnished free meeting space for the legislators and won the honor.

The state's first legislators met here from June 1821 through October 1826, when the new Capitol was ready in Jefferson City. Today, the Missouri Department of Natural Resources gives tours of the fully restored first Capitol, where frontiersmen and scholars alike met atop the Peck Brothers General Store. Tours are available Monday through Saturday every hour. The First Missouri State Capitol is located at 200 S. Main. Call (314) 946-9282 for more information.

There are also many interesting buildings throughout town. In the basement of 318 South Main Street there are bars on the windows and pegs in the wall, because this is the site of Missouri's first prison. The house at 724 South Main Street was the local presidential campaign headquarters for Abraham Lincoln.

The Lewis and Clark Center Museum is also worth a look. It is located at 701 Riverside Drive, or call (314) 947-3199 for tour information. On your way out, the riverfront park's winding path takes you past the restored train depot and numerous benches, offering a great view of the Missouri River and a perfect way to round out the afternoon.

The St. Charles Convention and Visitors Bureau has several free brochures, which include histories on specific parts of town. The bureau also publishes an eco-tourism series of free booklets on hiking, bicycling, bird watching and a fall leaves tour of St. Charles county.

Annual events include the Lewis and Clark Rendezvous the third weekend of May; the Festival of the Little Hills the third weekend in August; Ragfest each Labor Day; a bluegrass festival each September; and both the Missouri River Storytelling Festival and Oktoberfest each October. Contact the St. Charles Visitors Center, 230 South Main Street, or call 1 (800) 366-2427, for more information.

Bed & Breakfasts

Boone's Lick Trail Inn	Loccoco House II B & B
(314) 947-7000	(314) 946-0619
Historic Main B & B	Sage House B & B
(314) 940-8847	(314) 947-4843
Lady B's B & B	St. Charles House Elegant B & B
(314) 947-3421	(314) 946-6221

Bike Rental
Touring Cyclist • 104 South Main Street • (314) 949-9630

CAVERN SPRINGS WINERY

300 Water Street, St. Charles, MO 63301
(314) 947-1200
Hours of Operation:
Monday through Saturday 10 a.m. to 6 p.m., Sunday noon to 6 p.m.

HOW TO GET THERE: Located one block west of the Historic District of St. Charles. Take I-70 to the St. Charles Fifth Street Exit. Go north to Boonslick Road, turn right. Turn left on Main Street and then left on Water Street.

Cavern Springs Winery is two blocks from the Missouri River, just on the edge of St. Charles' historic district. Cavern Springs is not your typical winery visit. Other than a single row of display vines, there is no vineyard here. The highlight of this stop is the fine dining and a history that is as far reaching as the underground cellar system, which extends close to a mile underneath St. Charles' bustling streets.

Several cellars here date back to 1851, when a Prussian brew master opened the Spring Brewery. To construct the cellars, workers used more than 1.3 million handmade bricks to construct the caverns and then cover them with the hill. There are still three existing brewmaster homes that form a triangle around the winery, presumably connected by several unexcavated cellars. The expansive cellars were also used for the first ice house and cannery west of the Mississippi.

"[The cellar] even produces its own weather patterns down here," said director Christopher Roussin. "Sometimes a dense fog will form."

This property was once owned by such notables as the first governor of Missouri, Alexander McNair, the son of Daniel Boone, Edward and the "Earl of Spencer" Robert Spencer (Princess Di's family) from the 1780s to the 1840s.

Beer was produced on the site until 1972 when the Van Dyke Brewery closed. The building lay dormant until Cavern Springs Winery opened in 1993. Now it houses a fine restaurant and winery.

Cavern Springs specializes in premium quality wines in a wide range of styles and varieties from dry to semi-sweet. Limited quantities are produced to assure the highest standards of quality. The vintner is Tony Kooyumjian, the owners are James Reid Sr. and James Reid Jr. and the president is Mark Milburn.

The original redwood vats are on display. Three freshwater springs flow into the cellars, supplying 50,000 gallons a day of fresh spring water to the location. The antique decor includes antique stained glass windows and the Morgan Club bar, which is 125-years-old. There are daily tours of the cellars and brewery.

CAVERN SPRINGS WINE LIST

Current Offerings:
BLANCHETTE: A sweet white wine made from Seyval Blanc grapes.
DUCHESNE: The Pinot Noir give this robust red its hearty burgundy flavor.
HARVEST RED: A sweet, fruity and full-bodied red wine from Pinot Noir grapes.
MERRIWEATHER: Semi-sweet white made from Johannesburg Riesling grapes.
PROPRIETOR'S RESERVE: Dry and crisp, from Johannesburg Riesling grapes.
SEYVAL BLANC: From Seyval Blanc grapes, this wine is a gold medal winner and named "Missouri's Best Wine" from the Eastern International Wine Competition.
SPRING BLUSH: Semi-sweet, light rose-colored wine. Fruity wine produced from Seyval Blanc and Chambourcin grapes.

At left, the historic vaulted cellars beneath Cavern Springs Winery. Above, the modern facade of one of Missouri's more urban wineries.

WINERY OF THE LITTLE HILLS

501 South Main Street, St. Charles, MO 63301
(314) 946-9339
Hours of Operation:
Sunday through Thursday 11 a.m. to 9 p.m.
Friday and Saturday 11 a.m. to 10 p.m.

HOW TO GET THERE: Located in the Historic District of St. Charles on South Main Street. Take I-70 to the St. Charles Fifth Street Exit. Go north to Boonslick Road and turn right. Take Boonslick to Riverfront Drive.

On the cobblestone Main Street of historic St. Charles, the Winery of the Little Hills has a shop and restaurant open year-round. The outdoor wine garden is an excellent place to enjoy lunch and a Missouri wine.

A winery was founded at this location in 1860 by the Wepprich family. Through the years it's been a pharmacy, meat locker and processing plant and is rumored to have served as a base for whiskey bootleggers during Prohibition.

Over a century later, Martha and Tony Kooyumjian reopened the winery. Today their focus is the restaurant, though the winery continues to bottle enough of its own champagne to still be considered a bonded winery. Unfortunately, the cellars are not open for tours.

They do offer their own award-winning wine list. All production and bottling is done at Augusta Winery. In addition to their own special line of wine, Winery of the Little Hills currently offers 13 other varieties of wines, including the renowned Missouri Valley White, winner of the Missouri State Fair Gold Medal two years in a row. Traditional sausage, cheese and crackers can be purchased to complement the wines, so stop to enjoy the shaded wine garden. A Winery of the Little Hills specialty is Alpenglow, a spiced wine that is usually served hot, with a cinnamon stick and a slice of orange or lemon.

While you're here, be sure and stop for an old-time portrait across the street at The Tintype Photo Parlour, 510 S. Main Street, (314) 925-2155. The clothes fit over your clothes, so there's no changing. Within minutes you'll be transformed into visions of your great grandparents, the Civil War era, prairie pioneers or Victorian-period style. Their motto is "We don't make you look better, we just make you look old."

WINERY OF THE LITTLE HILLS
WINE LIST

Current Offerings:

ALPENGLOW	PINK CATAWBA
BLACKBERRY	PIONEER
CHAMBOURCIN	PORT
CHANCELLOR BLANC	SEYVAL OAK
CONCORD	SPRING ROSÉ
GRAPE JUICE	SPUMANTE BLUSH
HERMANNSBERGER	SPUMANTE GOLDEN
MISSOURI CHAMPAGNE	STEINBERG
MISSOURI VALLEY RED	VIDAL OAK
MISSOURI VALLEY WHITE	VIDAL
NORTON	VIGNOLES

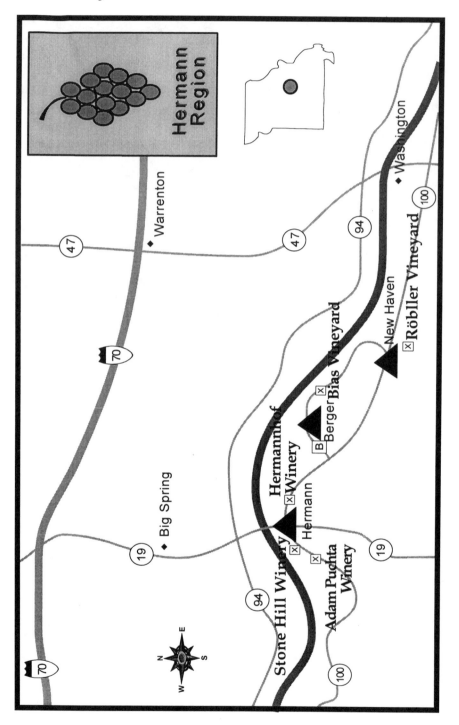

HERMANN REGION

The Hermann wine region is set within the heart of the Missouri Rhineland. It includes Adam Puchta Winery, Hermannhof Winery, Stone Hill Wine Company, Bias Vineyard & Winery and Röbller Vineyard.

Touring this region will take you through the northern most rolling hills of the Ozark Plateau. You'll visit Missouri's biggest winery, and some of the smaller ones, as well as one of the most recent additions to the industry. Maifest and Oktoberfest are also celebrated by many of the wineries in this section.

EXPLORING HERMANN

Adam Puchta Winery, Hermannhof Winery, Stone Hill Winery

B & Bs • Bikes • Camping • Crafts • Eats • Gas • Lodging • Parking
Post Office • Restrooms • RV Park
Visitors Center, 306 Market Street, Hermann, MO 65041, 1 (800) 932-8687

Hermann was founded by German settlers in 1836 and soon attained world-wide acclaim for its wines. Even today Hermann, located on the southern bank of the Missouri River, remains the hub of Missouri wine production. At one time Hermann was home to 65 wineries, with 40 more dotted along the river valley nearby. Today there are several wineries, including Missouri's largest and most awarded winery, Stone Hill.

Even those not interested in wine will enjoy a visit to Hermann with its rich history and many festivals that celebrate its German heritage. *Midwest Living Magazine* said it best, "Hermann . . . more German than some cities in Germany."

Hermannites raise their children using "the Hermann formula: the first year wine, the second year wine and sauerkraut."

Hermann was founded in 1836 by the German Settlement Society of Philadelphia, whose members were disheartened at the loss of native customs and language among their countrymen in America. This "Second Fatherland" was intended to be a self-supporting refuge for German heritage and tradition. The proposed community was set up as a joint-stock company and was advertised throughout the United States and Germany. The colony quickly attracted a variety of professionals, artisans and laborers, drawn by the idea of a "German Athens of the West."

On behalf of the society, one member acquired 11,300 acres of Frene Creek valley land for $15,612. His choice for the site, bounded by hills and bluffs on three sides and the Missouri River on the north and teeming with wild grapevines, was apparently influenced by its similarity to the Rhine River region in Germany.

Anxious to begin on what they expected to become one of the largest cities in the United States, the German Settlement Society modeled the layout of the colony on that of Philadelphia. Selecting the name of Germany's national hero, Hermann (Arminius in Latin), who defeated the Roman legion in 9 A.D., seemed a fitting symbol for the great dream their new settlement embodied.

By 1852, more than 470 acres of vineyards were in production around Hermann. By the turn of the century, Stone Hill was the third largest winery in the world (second in the United States), producing 1,250,000 gallons a year and winning international gold medals.

Today, Hermann is again home to the largest winery in the state (Stone Hill) and is once again vigorously making wine. Close to 200 acres of grapes again grow on the hills around Hermann and the German heritage of Hermann is as strong as ever. Hermannhof Winery has also been awarded the Brown-Forman Trophy for Best New World White Wine.

Almost every weekend during the summer months, Hermann plays host to some sort of German festival. The biggest ones are Maifest and October Weekends. The Visitors Center will give you the exact dates. Festivities include traditional German dancing, brats, beer, wine and yodelling. After all, it was the Germans who believed that Sunday's duties included not only church, but revelry after a hard week of work.

Be sure and visit a few of Hermann's countless antique shops. My personal favorite is John and Mae Wilding's Red Barn Craft Shop and Gallery, located at 523 West 9th Street. Call (573) 486-5544 for more information.

In Hermann, there is simply too much to see in one day, so take your cue to stay in one of Hermann's many bed & breakfasts. Hermann's Garden Club has also started garden tours. Call Alice Calhoun for details (573) 486-3060.

Say hello to the Pied Piper while munching on some good bratwurst.

Hermann is home to many annual festivals, including Maifest, Oktoberfest and the Grape Stomp (shown below).

Bed & Breakfasts

There are umpteen B & Bs in Hermann. Call the Visitor Information Center at (573) 486-2744 to book a reservation, or for more information.

Alice's Wharf Street B & B
(573) 486-5785

Angels in the Attic
(573) 486-5037 or 1 (888) 264-3553

Aunt Flora's Summerhouse
(573) 486-3591

Bide-A-Wee B & B Inn
(573) 486-3961

Birk's Gasthaus
(573) 486-2911

Captain Wohlt Inn
(573) 486-3357

A Country Farm B & B
(573) 564-8001 or (573) 252-4591

Die Gillig Heimat
(573) 943-6942

Drei Madelhaus
(573) 486-3552

Edelweiss B & B
(573) 486-3184

Esther's Ausblick
(573) 486-2170

Gatzemeyer Guest House
(573) 486-2635

Grandma Linda's B & B
(573) 486-2894

Hammock Hollow Farm
(573) 486-5851

Hermann Hill Vineyard & Inn
(573) 486-4455

John Bohlken Inn
(573) 486-3903

Kolbe Guest Haus
(573) 486-3453

A Little Log Cabin In The Woods
(573) 252-4301

Market Street B & B
(573) 486-5597

Mary Elizabeth House
(573) 486-3281

Meyer's Fourth Street B & B
(573) 486-2917

Meyer's Hilltop Farm
(573) 486-5778

Mumbrauer Gasthaus
(573) 486-5246

Nestle Inn
(573) 486-5893

Patty Kerr B & B
(573) 486-2510

Pelze Nichol Haus B & B
(573) 486-3886

Reiff House
(573) 486-2994 or 1 (800) 482-2994

Schmidt Guesthouse
(573) 486-2146

Season to Season
(573) 486-3596

Steeple View
(573) 486-3086

Strassner Suites
(573) 486-2682

White House Hotel 1868
(573) 486-3200 or (573) 486-3493

Deutschheim State Historic Site

Deutschheim State Historic Site preserves Missouri's early German heritage. Tour guides share insights into what life was like for German immigrants in the 19th century. They explain why and how the Germans came, and what they brought with them.

Deutschheim is a museum comprised of the Pommer-Gentner House and the Strehly House and Winery. Tours include the residence, the attached winery and the print shop. The Strehly House was the site of the first print shop in Hermann, and the German newspaper *Lichtfreund* (Friend of Light) was published in the ground floor shop. "But his four plus acres [of grapes] brought him a better income than his newspaper and printing business ever did," said site administrator Dr. Erin Renn.

Within these historic buildings are antique porcelains, furniture, the Midwest's earliest surviving carved wine cask (dated 1875), wooden clogs, early German furniture and a variety of arts and crafts from the past.

Four tours a day begin at 109 West Second Street, for a nominal fee. Call (573) 486-2200 for details.

How to get there: Go west on Second Street to 109 West Second Street.

Deutschheim features an early carved wine barrel and these early grape vines, believed to have been planted in the early 1830s. According to site administrator Erin Renn, Ph.D. (pictured) Hermann's original land grants included free land for settlers who promised to grow grapes for at least seven years.

In 1995, Oktoberfest Became October Weekends

After Hermann's month-long festival in 1994, many locals were feeling like it was time for changes to be made. Over the years the crowds had become more unmanageable as a whole, and were deterring visitors who wanted to celebrate Hermann's German heritage more quietly. During the late 1980s, the Hermann Police Department were arresting 300 people on alcohol-related charges in October. An estimated 100,000 came in 1994.

Stone Hill Winery, which founded the festival in 1970, said it would no longer participate in Oktoberfest. Mayor John Bartel supported the action. The Hermann Vintners Association also agreed to change its promotion strategy.

"We have made every effort possible to control over consumption," Stone Hill's Jim Held said. "But when large groups of people arrive in town already intoxicated, we are left with only one choice."

"We just want to attract people," Held said, "who appreciate our winery and the town of Hermann for their beauty and historic significance."

In 1994 the Missouri Highway Patrol said the festival caused bumper-to-bumper traffic along roads from Hermann to Interstates 44 and 70.

"Any time you have extra traffic and extra drinking, you have concerns. We've had accidents in the past that we can attribute to the partygoers at the Oktoberfest. You can't blame that on Oktoberfest, you have to blame that on the people who go down there and use alcohol to excess."

The Rhineland "Wurstjaegers" dance throughout the year at German festivals.

In 1995 changes were made: "Oktoberfest" became "October in Hermann." Visitors were asked to come sober, stay civilized and enjoy the sights and special events.

Alhough the other wineries made no efforts to limit the number of visitors, Stone Hill restricted its visitors by as many as 50,000 over the four weekends, when it sold tickets in advance and required them for admittance to its events. Local businesses also began trying to promote Hermann beyond just festival time.

These changes led to positive results for the most part. Many storeowners said business was as good as last year or in some cases better, though others said sales had decreased. Few problems were reported with the crowd.

The Hermann Police Department made only 43 alcohol-related arrests in October 1995. Even the third week of the festival, during which as many as 100 arrests have been made over three days in previous years, only 14 were made.

In 1994 Hermann Mayor John Bartel said, "I think you could say that on a couple weekends our cup runneth over."

One year later Bartel said, "We never have a problem with people who want to come and have a good time and enjoy Hermann. When it got to the point, though, where other people were having a good time with no respect for other people's privacy and freedoms, things needed to change."

Compiled from the Associated Press *and the* Columbia Daily Tribune

A n n u a l   E v e n t s

March: Wurstfest
May: Maifest—third week in May
June: Annual Quilt Show
July: Cajun Concert on the Hill
August: Great Stone Hill Grape Stomp
October: October Weekends
December: Christmas Park of Dreams & Kristkindl Market

Vicki Puchta

ADAM PUCHTA WINERY

Route 1, Box 73, Hermann, MO 65041
(573) 486-5596
Hours of Operation:
Monday through Saturday 10 a.m. to 6 p.m.
Sunday 11 a.m. to 6 p.m.

HOW TO GET THERE: Puchta Winery is located 2 miles southwest of Hermann off Highway 100. Follow the signs to Frene Creek County Road.

Puchta Winery is considered "Hermann's newest old winery." Tim Puchta (pronounced POOK-tah) is the sixth generation in the line of John Henry Puchta, who immigrated to this homestead in 1839. John Henry ran a commercial vineyard here from 1855 to 1919. Prohibition shut him down, and it was Tim who reopened the winery in 1990.

Tim was a respiratory therapist at Columbia Regional Hospital before getting

his hands full-time into vines and wines. He continued working at the hospital for several years while he got his winery going, and has never looked back.

"This has been a goal of mine for many, many years," Tim said. "I've always loved wine and I'm a farm boy at heart. I love working at home . . . it leaves time to be with my kids."

Tim and Vicki Puchta's success would surely receive a nod from their winemaking ancestors. The winery has received 17 awards in just the last 5 years.

Today, Tim and Vicki, along with a few workers produce up to 8,000 gallons of wine a year. They have 3 acres of Norton, which are 6 years old, and purchase the rest.

"But we don't have any large-scale plans. I want to keep the ambiance of the farm intact. I don't need a Mercedes. A 4x4 Ford truck suits me just fine," Tim said. "According to research, the most profitable wineries seem to be at the 15,000 to 25,000 gallon level, so that's where we're heading."

As Tim quickly pointed out though, as you're growing, you're constantly updating equipment. Trying to grow a business produces its own problems, what, with juggling the books and keeping your livelihood healthy on the vine.

"This isn't like a grain crop. There's a lot of overhead. You spend about $8,000 an acre in the first year for posts, irrigation and vines. Then you wait 4 to 7 years to crop that. Then, for a dry red, you age it in a barrel for 2 years. And remember—

that's all before you make dollar one. It's about 10 to 15 years before the break-even point."

And then there's the X factor—the inevitable twist that defies planning. Today, Tim is in the field inspecting his vines, which, without warning, dropped all of their leaves earlier this week. "I don't know what happened. Everything defoliated. Now the secondary leaves are going to get burnt," he said. Tim suspects that herbicide from a neighboring farmer's field has drifted over his vineyard. But he's too busy pruning to dwell on how that will affect his grape production.

"Yeah, I remember being told in 1990 there was no reason to plant [grapes], because there's enough," Tim said, shaking his head. "Since then, though, the industry has grown so rapidly that demand has exceeded supply. No one anticipated such an increase in sales." This means it's harder for smaller wineries to compete, since larger wineries often end up with the lion's share of the harvest.

Another day of hard work lies ahead, as Tim juggles countless variables. As I walk down the hill, into view of the tasting room, I see their sons playing outside, pushing their Tonka trucks around a dirt-mound city. A dozen puppies yip from a pen nearby. Tall oaks are shading the tasting room and the wine cellar, and I see those worn steps trod by his great-great-grandfather Adam Puchta.

As I walk away, I reflect on Tim's hard work, and how he shirked his 9 to 5 job for this demanding lifestyle . . . and I'm thinking to myself, I wouldn't be looking back either.

ADAM PUCHTA
WINE LIST

Spencer Puchta

ADAM'S CHOICE: German-style semi-dry white wine.

BELLANDAIS: Dry, lightly oaked red wine similar to a light Pinot Noir.

HUNTER'S RED: Blended Chianti-style red, light and fruity.

MISTY VALLEY WHITE: Semi-sweet white wine.

NORTON: Dry, oak-aged red wine, similar to a Merlot.

PRIVATE RESERVE SEYVAL: Dry barrel-aged Chardonnay-style white.

REIFENSTAHLER: Sweet red wine.

VIDAL: Dry Sauvignon Blanc-style white wine.

VIGNOLES: Semi-sweet white wine with strawberry and kiwi tones.

VIVANT: Fruity, off-dry white with tropical fruit flavors.

HERMANNHOF WINERY

330 East First Street, Hermann, MO 65041
(573) 486-5959 or 1 (800) 393-0100
Hours of Operation:
Monday through Saturday 10 a.m. to 5 p.m.
Sundays 11 a.m. to 5 p.m. Closed major holidays.

HOW TO GET THERE: Take Highway 19 across the bridge into Hermann. Immediately on the south side of the river, head east on Highway 100 about a mile. Hermannhof is on the south side of the street, on the eastern edge of town. When leaving town watch the posted speed limit—this is a notorious speed trap.

Located on the eastern, "French" edge of town, Hermannhof turned from dream to reality in 1848, when construction began. Hermannhof has been producing wine on and off since 1852, except for the years of prohibition. The estate was later used as a brewery by Kropp Brewery, then turned into apartments—its intricate series of 10 underground cellars filled with rubbish—until the property was revived under the guidance of owners James and Mary Dierberg. In its most recent evolution, the century-old stone and brick building is once again serving as the foundation for the winemaking art that began so long ago.

With 16 years of experience, Paul LeRoy is the resident vintner. At peak harvest times he oversees a staff of 30 people. They produce about 20,000 gallons of wine annually, 1,500 of which is champagne. LeRoy's expertise guided Hermannhof to a recent award of "Best New World White Wine," for their Vignoles.

Hermannhof's tour guide takes you through century-old production cellars and explains today's state-of-the-art equipment.

This took place at the New World International Wine Competition in 1997. Judge Jerry Mead summed it up in his newsletter: *Mead on Wine*. (When reading the following excerpt, keep in mind he's addressing people who think there's nothing between the East and West coast, but desert, cows and hay bales.)

"Knowing the winner of the Brown-Forman Trophy for Best New World White Wine won't do you much good unless you live in Missouri. I'm not kidding. For the second time in recent years, a Missouri wine produced from a grape called Vignoles (a French-American hybrid) has walked away with this trophy. Hermannhof Winery's 1995 'Missouri' Vignoles is just off-dry, with pleasant fruit and a very long finish. It's not too sweet for food, nor too dry for casual sipping."

As with other Hermann wineries, the vineyards are located outside of town. The sights and sounds of exploring this winery do, however, continue below ground. For the price of a hotdog you can tour the historic wine cellars, which have been home to winemakers, brew masters and even a wedding. As you tour the cellars 15 feet below ground, you can feel the vibrations as the Amtrak trains rush by only 100 feet away. The tour continues into the modern age, as your tour guide shows you the monolithic, stainless steel cooling tanks that may be producing tomorrow's award winners.

Once you're back up top, visit the smokehaus and sample their selection of fine wines, cheeses, breads and sausages. The winery's *weinstube* deli is open for lunch so be sure to picnic under the grape pergola or in the shade of the gazebo.

Hermannhof's vast Festhalle, located across the street just west of the main building, is used for all sorts of activities, including larger-than-life wine tastings, receptions and, of course, bratwurst-swinging, wine-drinking festivals.

HERMANNHOF WINE LIST

Current Offerings:

BARREL FERMENTED SEYVAL: Smooth, rich and elegant. Buttery, fruity aromas and flavors dominate with hints of oak and cream lingering on the finish.

BRUT RESERVE

CABERNET SAUVIGNON: A rich varietal aroma with flavors of berries, black cherries and spicy oak.

CHERRY: A sweet wine produced with ripe, slowly-fermented Wisconsin cherries.

FOUNDERS RESERVE: A lighter style dry red with delicate characters of berries and spice.

ICEWINE: Sweet and rich, with spicy fruit flavors.

IMPERIAL CUVEE: Delicate and fruity champagne, with a fresh yeasty creaminess in the nose and subtle apple-pear flavors balanced by a firm acidity and distinct note of sweetness.

NORTON: Deep ruby, medium-bodied. Moderately tannic. Brown spice, black pepper and plums. Balanced and flavorful. Powerful oak elements add complexity, while bold acids elevate the entire structure.

SPRING BLUSH: Light and fresh.

VIDAL BLANC: Finished dry and aged "sur-lie" for six months.

VIGNOLES: Semi-sweet and fruity, with citrus flavors and a crisp, lively acidity.

WHITE LADY: This bright semi-dry, Rhine-style white is a perennial best-seller.

STONE HILL WINERY

Route 1, Box 26, Hermann, MO 65041
1 (800) 909-WINE (9463)
Hours of Operation:
Monday through Saturday 8:30 a.m. to Dusk
Sundays 11 a.m. to 6 p.m.

HOW TO GET THERE: Take I-70 to Highway 19 and go south. Or take I-44 to Highway 19 north. Basically, if you travel Highway 19 between I-70 and I-44 you will run into Hermann. Once there, take Highway 100 west and follow the signs.

Established in 1847, Stone Hill Winery was once the third largest winery in the world. Today, it is the largest winery in the state and the third most awarded winery in America. In 1995, Stone Hill produced close to 40 percent of Missouri's wine. Annual production is 150,000 gallons of wine.

Wine production reached its peak at Stone Hill around the turn of the century, only to be cut short 20 years later by Prohibition. During this dark time in Stone Hill's history, the arched underground wine cellars were used to cultivate mushrooms. These cellars are the largest series of underground, vaulted cellars in America.

The once grand winery was rescued in 1965 by Jim and Betty Held. Jim says the family started the business with "nothing but determination." Along with their four children, they moved from a nearby hog farm and borrowed $1,500 to finance their first grape crush. They moved in on the second floor and began the long process of restoring its picturesque buildings and vaulted cellars. It took considerable investments of time and money, but rewards and proof of their progress came along the way. Their winemaker, Dave Johnson, was named national "Winemaker of the Year," and in 1982 Stone Hill was Missouri's Small Business of the Year. The Held family was also named "Wine Growing Family of the Year" in 1996 at a national event sponsored by *Vineyard and Winery Management Magazine.*

With three of the Held children now holding degrees in enology and viticulture, the winery today is once again earning international attention. During the past three years alone, the winery has won 414 national and international wine awards.

At vineyards just outside of town, Stone Hill grows American hybrid grapes to produce wines that are similar to the ever-popular Chardonnay and Sauvignon Blanc. However, the pride of Stone Hill is their Norton. Stone Hill also took the Governor's Cup in 1995. Their late-harvest Vignoles won first in the off-dry white wine class. The top three winning wineries were Stone Hill Winery with 15, St. James Winery with 12 and Mount Pleasant Winery with 8 awards.

The Helds and their staff are planning to increase their vineyard from 80 acres to 104 in the future and also add a couple new varieties of grapes to their repertoire. Overseeing this development is Katie Nott. At 22 she's one of the youngest and one of the few female vineyard managers in the country. A native of Michigan, Katie came to Stone Hill in May of 1996 as an intern from Michigan State University.

Betty and Jim Held are largely responsible for the rebirth of Missouri's wine industry.

Dave Johnson "thiefs" a sample of Norton from a barrel in Stone Hill's Apostle Cellar.

Vintner Profile:
Dave Johnson

After 19 years of working with the Held family to improve the winery and vineyards, Dave has become the most awarded American winemaker outside of California—and only two winemakers there have garnered more medals than Dave in the past five years. It's quite an achievement—not only because of the esteemed competition, but also because few people west of the Rockies have ever even heard of some of the grape varieties grown in Missouri.

Dave Johnson, vintage 1979.

Q. What wines do you feel represent Missouri best?

A. I guess you could say Norton is *the* Missouri red. Vignoles is another variety that seems to please the wine judges.

Q. So, have you seen the best of these wines?

A. I've never made a wine yet in which I couldn't see at least a little room for improvement. We have the proper equipment to make it well at the winery, but we can fine-tune it in the vineyards . . . it will take some time, but we *will* improve both the Norton and the Vignoles.

Q. What are your biggest obstacles?

A. Our weather here makes grape growing a challenge. Another problem here is a lack of a labor force. With an unemployment rate of less than 1 percent in Hermann, we *must* mechanize our vineyards as much as possible.

Q. What are you most proud of?

A. Well, it's been gratifying to receive so much attention on wines like Norton and Vignoles, but I'm very happy with the success we've had on our sweet wines. Many other wineries treat their sweet wines like second-class citizens, but I pay as much attention to my Concord and Pink Catawba as I do the Norton.

Stone Hill is listed on the National Historic Register and offers full tours of its antique cellars and state-of-the-art production facility. Stone Hill has also expanding its tasting room and gift shop. Be sure and stop at the Vintage 1842 Restaurant, which specializes in European fare and is housed in a renovated carriage house and horse barn.

STONE HILL WINE LIST

Current Offerings:

BARREL FERMENTED SEYVAL: Fermented and aged in small French oak barrels to develop richness and complexity. Dry and full-bodied. Best of show and gold medal winner in the dry white category at the Missouri State Fair.

BLUSH: Stone Hill's version of a White Zinfandel. A bit lighter and more delicate than a traditional rosé. Light and fruity. Silver medal winner at the International Eastern Wine Competition.

CONCORD GRAPE JUICE: Naturally sweet pure grape juice.

CONCORD: Bursting with the sweet, robust flavor of ripe Missouri Concord grapes. Winner of the silver medal at the San Diego National Wine Competition.

GOLDEN RHINE: A semi-sweet, traditional German-style white wine, with a fruity aroma and flavor. Winner of the silver medal at the Missouri State Fair.

GOLDEN SPUMANTE: Rich, fruity and semi-sweet. Winner of the gold medal and best of show at the Missouri State Fair.

HERMANNSBERGER: This semi-dry red wine was blended as a sister to the Steinberg. Fruity like a Beaujolais. Winner of the silver medal at the World Wine Championships in Chicago.

MISSOURI CHAMPAGNE: This Stone Hill champagne is naturally fermented in the bottle, riddled by hand in the traditional French method after aging on the yeast. Crisp and delicate, this Brut-style champagne is made from 100 percent Vidal grapes. Winner of the silver medal at the Missouri State Fair.

NORTON (Estate bottled blue label): A very dry, full-bodied, oak-aged red wine that has won national and international awards.

NORTON (Red label): This medium-bodied, dry red wine has a beautiful deep color and distinctive Norton varietal character, with just a touch of toasty oak. With its soft tannins, this lighter-styled Norton can be enjoyed while young, or allowed to develop in the bottle for two to five years. Silver medal winner at the World Wine Championships, Chicago.

PINK CATAWBA: Light, sweet and full of the famous Catawba flavor.

PORT: This vintage-style port is produced in limited quantities. Matured in oak casks, this rich dark port can be enjoyed now, or left to develop in the bottle for many years. The 1992 port was selected as the best American port by the *Wine Enthusiast Magazine,* proving that ports made from the Norton grape can compete with the best. Bronze medal winner at the California Farmers Fair.

ROSÉ MONTAIGNE: A semi-sweet rosé that is soft and mellow with a touch of sweetness and a lovely floral aroma. Winner of the silver medal at the San Diego National Wine Competition.

Hermann Region

SEYVAL: A fruity, dry white wine with excellent varietal character. Similar in style to a fruity Chardonnay. This wine is Stone Hill's best-selling varietal wine. It has won national and international wine competitions, including the gold medal at the San Diego National Wine Competition.

SPARKLING GRAPE JUICE: Sparkling, naturally sweet, non-alcoholic grape juice.

SPARKLING RASPBERRY JUICE: A light, non-alcoholic raspberry-flavored juice.

SPUMANTE BLUSH: Bubbling wine with a distinctive pink color and fruity flavor. Winner of the gold medal at the Los Angeles County Fair.

STEINBERG: Stone Hill's best-seller. A delicate, semi-dry, German-style white wine vinted from fine European hybrid grape varieties. A gold medal winner at the Missouri State Fair.

VIDAL: A dry, white varietal wine that has a delicate fruit and herbal aroma with just a touch of oak. Bronze medal winner at the California Farmer's Fair.

VIGNOLES: This rich, semi-sweet wine has a natural residual sugar and a varietal flavor. Winner of the gold medal at the San Diego National Wine Competition.

Be Sure to Explore Nearby Cajun Country

W hile you're out exploring, look for the River Landing Restaurant and Ferry in Fredricksburg, Missouri. Located west of Hermann off Highway 100, this ferry ride takes you across the Gasconade River and drops you at a fine Cajun restaurant.

The River's Edge Restaurant menu takes you back to the bayou. A wide array of Cajun food and seafood is offered including Cajun catfish, charbroiled shrimp, barbecued ribs, crab legs, swordfish and blackened T-bone steaks. Prices range from $8 to $15. For less than $30, here's the real Cajun deal: The Cajun Crab Boil for two. It includes a pound of crabs, a half-pound of shrimp, a half-pound of crawfish, two baked potatoes, two ears of corn, gumbo and plenty of napkins! River's Edge also make their own sauces, from barbecue to poppy seed salad dressings. Call (573) 294-7207 for more information.

The *Roy J* ferry operates on an *as needed* basis. Operator Junior Deppe will come get you when you pull up to the river. Junior has been doing this for ten years. The ferry carries two cars with room left over for all of the local porch dogs looking for a little adventure themselves. Charges are $2 one way or $3 round-trip.

Canoe and Jon boat rentals are also available. Call (573) 294-7203 for information.

HOW TO GET THERE: Fredricksburg is so small, they don't have an address. From Hermann, take Highway 100 west 6 miles to Route J. Take Route J for 8 miles. You'll come to the Gasconade River.

EXPLORING BERGER
Bias Vineyards and Winery

Eats • Parking • Restrooms

Instead of a flashy Chamber of Commerce billboard like you see at the edge of some towns, here there's just a leaning old barn held up by God-only-know's. The suburbs are a block from downtown and then you're in farmland.

But Berger wasn't always this big. The area that we call Berger today was originally home to the Shawnee Indians. Then in 1790 two Frenchmen, the Bershay brothers, settled in the area. German immigrants soon followed. The town of Berger was established in 1818 and incorporated in 1928. American settlers primarily came from the Kentucky and Virginia areas. Berger was one of the first European settlements in Franklin County. The current population is 247.

The St. Paul Church is one of three churches
found in this tiny community.

BIAS VINEYARDS & WINERY

3166 Highway B, P.O. Box 93, Berger, MO 63014

(573) 834-5475

Hours of Operation:

Summer: Monday through Saturday 10 a.m. to 6 p.m.

Sunday 11 a.m. to 6 p.m.

Fall and Winter: Monday through Saturday 10 a.m. to 5 p.m.

Sunday 11 a.m. to 5 p.m.

HOW TO GET THERE: The winery and sales room are located on Route B, one mile east of Berger. From Hermann, take Highway 100 east 7 miles to Route B, then go north through Berger. Continue 1.5 miles and watch for their sign.

Located on a 64-acre farm high atop the bluffs overlooking the Missouri River valley, the laid back atmosphere, gorgeous scenery and friendly folks of Bias Vineyards & Winery make this a favorite stop for both locals and city-escapees.

The entrance to Bias Winery is a mile and a half past Berger, along a circuitous river bottom road. You cross over an old wooden bridge, go across the railroad tracks and up a steep hill. When you see the railroad tracks: Stop, Look and Listen. Two or three trains pass by here each hour, so stop and look both ways before crossing.

Despite its seemingly out-of-the-way location, the Bias Winery is hopping on sunny Saturdays and Sundays. Today is a day of rest and relaxation and

Jim Bias

everyone has taken their cues. The air of joviality is underscored by the 21 wine bottles draped with various awards and the meticulously cared-for vineyards nearby.

Cars bearing license plates of Missouri, Illinois, Iowa and New Mexico fill the parking lot. Modes of transportation range from a topless Jeep and a new Beemer, to wired-together farm trucks and a horse (no license plate to be seen).

Bias is a small, family-owned winery that intends to stay that way. Jim and Norma Bias established the Bias Winery in 1980, making it a relative newcomer to the list of Hermann-area winemakers. The Bias family started their winery with a 5-acre Catawba vineyard. They have since expanded with varieties of French hybrids including Chambourcin, DeChaunac, Seyval and Vidal.

The Bias family strives to make fresh, clean-tasting wine. Their wines are produced from their own 8-acre vineyard, located only 600 feet from the winery. This allows for prompt harvesting and crushing of the grapes at the moment they reach their peak ripeness. All of the grapes are harvested by hand from mid-August to mid-September. The pressing, fermentation, aging and bottling are all performed on the estate.

A sign in the tasting room says "Would you like to speak to the man in charge OR the woman who knows what's going on?" Both Bonnie Horstmann and Linda Sitton "know what's going on" and are informative guides to tasting the wide variety of Bias wines. Be sure and try the best-selling favorite "Weisser Flieder" (German for white lilac).

In addition to exploring the fine wines of Bias, a walk through the vineyards is a must. These vines are among the oldest, thickest and healthiest you'll see—as thick as your wrist. Many of these vines were planted in 1969. The thick loess soil, good sun exposure, amazing water and air drainage and the meticulous care by Donnie Blanton and Jim's son Jimmy Bias, with help from Bonnie Horstmann and Carol Bradley, make these vines look like something out of *Jack and the Beanstalk*. There is also a small cemetery here dating back to the early 1800s, just below the vineyards near a line of tall cedar trees.

And one last note: Beware of the "Sausage Sniper." This slow-moving old dog is easy enough to evade, but seems to end up with your sausage no matter what, given his slow but relentless attack and his telepathic powers.

BIAS WINE LIST

Current Offerings:
APPLE WINE
BERGER RED: Sweet red.
CHAMBOURCIN: Dry red.
CHANTILLY: Sweet red.
DE CHAUNAC: Dry red.
FROSTY MEADOW WHITE: Ice wine.
JUBILEE RED: Semi-sweet red.
JUBILEE WHITE: Semi-sweet white.
LIEBESWEIN: Semi-dry white.
MEAD: Sweet honey wine.
PINK CATAWBA: Sweet rosé.
PREMIUM RIVER VIEW WHITE:
Dry white.
PREMIUM VIDAL: Dry white.
RIVER BLUFF ROUGE: Semi-dry rosé.
RIVER VIEW WHITE: Dry white.
SCHÖNER FRÜHLING: Semi-dry white.
SEYVAL: Semi-dry white.
SPARKLING GRAPE JUICE
SPARKLING RASPBERRY JUICE
SUNSET RED: Sweet red.
SWEET AMBROSIA: Sweet white.
VICTORIAN RED: Sweet red.
VIGNOLES: Semi-dry white.
WEISSER FLIEDER: Sweet white.

Beware of the Sausage Sniper.

Annual Events

March: Wurstfest
April: Cajun Cook-off, Festival of the New Wines
May: Maifest
August: Pre-Harvest Festival
September: Chili Cook-off
October: Oktoberfest
November: Hayrides
December: Trim a Tree Party

EXPLORING NEW HAVEN
Röbller Vineyard & Winery

B & Bs • Eats • Lodging • Parking • Post Office • Restrooms
New Haven Chamber of Commerce: (573) 237-3830

Originally called Miller's Landing, New Haven was founded in 1836 on the south bank of the Missouri River. In the late 1800s, the town was a busy shipping center and bustled with activity brought by the riverboat traffic. Since then, river traffic has almost stopped—other than an occasional barge or jet-skier from Washington.

Today, a walk through downtown New Haven evokes the feeling you get when viewing a Norman Rockwell painting. In addition to historic homes, the downtown area also has several antique, gift and specialty shops, along with a fine restaurant.

Spend the day wandering the historic streets or head to the scenic Riverfront Park for an afternoon picnic in the gazebo. A visit to New Haven isn't complete without doing the "circuit." This includes eating a fine meal at Raymond's Restaurant and visiting the Röbller Vineyard, located just minutes away.

Raymond's Restaurant is the place to be after a long day of exploring Missouri wine country. Tons of old photos line the walls offering a pictorial history of the New Haven area, early railroad and river traffic, past fires, early Corps of Engineers crews attempting to control the Mighty Mo by weaving willow mats, and other early pictures you normally find tucked away in the corner of a museum.

Daily specials include mixed grilled shrimp and vegetables on a Portabello mushroom, and other fine eating pleasures created by Phil and Ray Jacobs. Entrees range from $8 to $16, and there is always a daily special. Raymond's has a full bar as well, and serves the locally produced Röbller wines in addition to other Missouri wines. Reservations are not required but are recommended for Friday and Saturday nights.

Bed & Breakfasts
The Welcome House I and II
(573) 237-2771

125 Front Street B & B
(573) 237-3534

Restaurant
Raymond's
(573) 237-7100

Governor Mel Carnahan presents Lois and Robert Mueller the
First Governor's Cup award for their Norton wine in 1993.

RÖBLLER VINEYARD & WINERY

275 Röbller Vineyard Road, New Haven, MO 63068

(573)237-3986

Hours of Operation:

Summer: Monday through Saturday 10 a.m. to 6 p.m.

Sunday noon to 6 p.m.

Winter: Monday through Saturday 11 a.m. to 5 p.m.

Sunday noon to 5 p.m.

HOW TO GET THERE: Röbller is located just off Highway 100, between Hermann and Washington. Take the Röbller Vineyard Road just east of the water tower. It's a gravel road that comes up quick—be watching for their small sign.

When you visit Röbller Vineyard & Winery, one of Missouri's newest wineries, you will find quality French hybrid varietal and traditionally styled blended wines that are sure to please. One Röbller wine you must sample is their Norton. This Native American red wine, with its well-balanced, mellow fruit, spices and soft tannins, is the most popular in their line.

The beautiful, rolling countryside here provides the perfect conditions for grape production while offering a spectacular view for the visitor. Like many vineyards in Missouri, Röbller is a family business. The husband and wife team of Robert and Lois Mueller own and operate the winery, with help from three of their children and other employees.

They produce about 4,000 gallons of wine annually but plan to increase their output with the planting of five more acres of vines, bringing the vineyard to

14 acres. Since its beginning in 1991, Röbller has been awarded the first Best of Show Governor's Cup for their Norton, along with several other awards that now line the tasting room.

Throughout the year, exciting events are held on the rolling terraces that surround the winery. On the Fourth of July weekend the winery hosts the BBQ and Blues Festival. In early August the energizing sounds of the Reggae Sunsplash Party stream through the air. The highlight of the year is the non-traditional Octoberfest Celebration which features live blues, jazz and reggae.

Depending on the season, you can watch the crew crushing, pressing, filtering and bottling—and don't forget to bring a kite to fly in the almost continual breeze. At night, the hills offer a great front row seat to a star-filled sky.

They also have some of the most inviting ad copy around: "I see in my mind a place . . . Where carefree is the only state of mind . . . Where an afternoon siesta among the fruited vines is not decay in values, but the rules to live by; Where the supreme conspiracy is the blurring of reality by nature's rolling landscape; Where time and reason become measures from a foreign world . . . It is a place you can only find on our map."

Röbller's vineyard specialist, Max Lawton.

The friendly folks at Röbller Vineyard & Winery are proud of the relaxed family atmosphere and are happy to play host to your entire family.

RÖBLLER WINE LIST
Current Offerings:

CHANCELLOR	SEYVAL
GABRIELLE'S BLUSH	SONATA
JEA d'EAU	ST. VINCENT
KASSELFEST	VIDAL
LE DUET	VIDAL BLANC
LE TROMPIER NOIR	VILLA ROUGE
NORTON	WHITE STEUBEN

Nearby: When you visit nearby Washington, be sure and visit the Gary Lucy Gallery at the corner of Main and Elm Streets. Lucy's passion in paint is America's inland waterways. His brilliant renditions of Missouri's glory days of river commerce come alive with his acute sense of light and life. If you've already been to Montelle Winery, you'll surely recognize his artwork on their wine label. Call the Lucy Gallery for more information at 1 (800) 937-4944.

Also, be sure to visit the Washington Art Fair and Winefest, which is held each May at the riverfront. About 4,000 people turn out for the tasting of 50 wines from nearby wineries. A small admission fee covers your wine drinking for the afternoon. Call (314) 239-1743 for more information and Amtrak schedules.

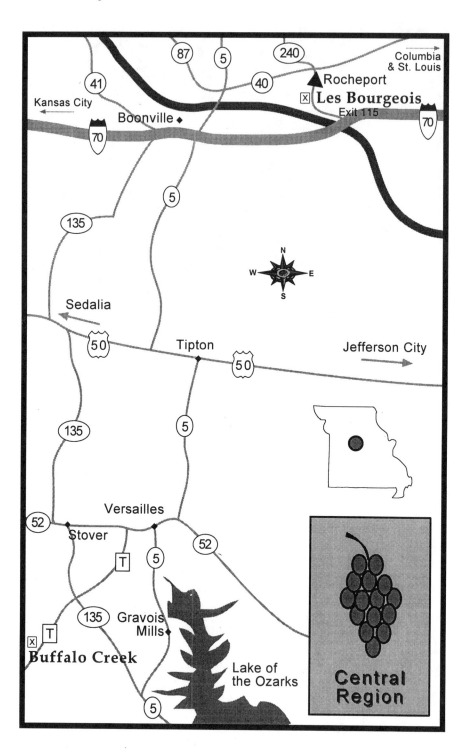

CENTRAL REGION

This region only includes two wineries, but they are two of my favorites. With its central location, Les Bourgeois Winery & Vineyards is a daytrip destination from almost anywhere in the state.You've probably driven past this winery many times. Located just 12 miles west of Columbia near I-70, Les Bourgeois commands one of the best views in the state. Towering limestone bluffs, the bend in the Missouri River and the Katy Trail meld their lines into a beautiful outdoor scene. If you've never driven across the Missouri River bridge between Boonville and Rocheport, you are in for a pleasant surprise.

Be sure to visit Stover, too. Jim Stephens at Buffalo Creek Vineyards & Winery is working on a tasting room with an equally gorgeous view overlooking the Lake of the Ozarks.

EXPLORING ROCHEPORT

Les Bourgeois Winery & Vineyards

Antiques • Bikes • Crafts • Entertainment • Eats • Gas
Historic Homes • Lodging • Post Office • Katy Trail State Park
Friends of Rocheport: (573) 698-3595

Rocheport offers many amenities for the Katy Trail user and is a popular starting point for many Sunday saunterers. Here you'll find many historic homes, nationally renowned antique shops, craft shops and cafés. One of the bed & breakfasts is a restored, 80-year-old schoolhouse, which was recently named one of the "Top 10 Most Romantic B & Bs in the U.S."

French for "port of rocks," Rocheport is better known today for its pleasant shopping district and historic flavor. With a population of 255, Rocheport entertains as many as 30,000 visitors annually. The local museum, (573) 698-7301, is an ideal place to recapture some of the early pioneer spirit. Open weekends from 1 p.m. to 4 p.m., it features artifacts and an extensive collection of black-and-white historical photographs.

The blackened ceiling of the Rocheport train tunnel is another reminder of the area's past. You can't say you've ridden the Katy Trail until you've passed through the MK&T tunnel, a 243-foot-long train tunnel built in 1893.

The towering limestone bluffs beside the Missouri River reflect another important aspect of Rocheport's history. The Moniteau bluffs are considered sacred by several tribes. "Moniteau" is a French derivative of "Manitou," the Indian word for Great Spirit, hence the naming of Moniteau Creek.

Thin strips of pewter shoot like ribbons from Harry Snyder's lathe as he uses hand-carved maple molds to turn flat sheets of pewter into bowls, plates and tankards. It takes about a day to turn out six bowls and another day to polish them.

The only pewtersmith west of the Mississippi, Harry offers a wide assortment of brilliant, usable pewter at his log shop in Rocheport. The Britannia alloy he uses has been safely used for dinnerware for more than 300 years.

The bluffs southeast of town bear a faded remnant of a Native American petroglyph. This is visible from the trail a few miles east of Rocheport above the Lewis and Clark cave, otherwise known as Torbett Spring. The maroon-colored petroglyph of a "V" with a dot is right beside the bottom edge of the left bow of a prominent fracture impression. The crescent moon and dot symbol is thought to signify water, thus indicating the water source below for fellow travelers.

The Lewis and Clark Expedition reported many "uncouth" murals and symbols upon the bluffs here, but couldn't examine them due to a severe infestation of rattlesnakes. Many were under overhanging bluffs that were summarily blasted off in later years to prevent train accidents.

Located on the Missouri River at the mouth of the Moniteau Creek, Rocheport grew rapidly as steamboat traffic increased. In 1849, 57 steamboats made 500 landings at Rocheport. That's more than one a day!

Though fires in 1892 and 1922 destroyed many historic buildings, Rocheport was placed on the National Register of Historic Places in 1976. Historic walking tours are offered April through October by the Friends of Rocheport. Call for a current schedule: (573) 698-3595.

Nearby: Missouri River City, at the I-70 Rocheport Exit 115, has antique and gift shops, a hotel and a play theater.

Bed & Breakfasts
Roby River Run B & B
(573) 698-2173

Schoolhouse B & B
(573) 698-2022

The Yates House B & B
(573) 698-2129

Bike Rental
Rocheport Cyclist
(573) 698-2043

Trailside Cafe &
Bike Rental
(573) 698-2702

Biking through the old MK&T Railroad tunnel is one of the highlights of the Katy Trail.

The new, oak-beamed bistro sits atop the bluffs overlooking the Missouri River.

LES BOURGEOIS
WINERY & VINEYARDS

P.O. Box 118, Rocheport, MO 65279
(573) 698-2133 or (573) 698-2300
Hours of Operation:
I-70 Winery & Gift Shop—daily 11 a.m. to 6 p.m.
Blufftop Bistro—Wednesday through Saturday 11 a.m. to 9 p.m.
and Sunday Brunch from 11 a.m. to 6 p.m.
A-frame Chalet—noon to sunset, March through October (50°F and over)

HOW TO GET THERE: Les Bourgeois has three locations, all right outside Rocheport. The winery and gift shop are just off I-70 at Exit 115; the new bistro and the original A-frame are just 1 mile north of I-70 on Route BB. Rocheport is 12 miles west of Columbia.

At the Les Bourgeois Winery & Vineyards you will find wonderful wine and great food coupled with a breathtaking panoramic view of the Missouri River bottoms.

"We've come a long way since 1985, when we had our garage declared a bonded winery, and used the A-frame as a tasting room," said founder, Curtis Bourgeois. "In those days, we did everything at our home, including pasting on the labels while we watched TV. We named our first wine 'Jeunette Rouge'—a Cajun word for a woman that means not quite old, not quite young, just right."

From a first year run of 500 gallons, to the opening of a tasting room in their A-frame five years later, the Bourgeois family has turned what started out as a part-time hobby into the fourth largest winery in Missouri, producing more than 200,000 bottles a year. These days, the garage is reserved for the sporty convertible, and a seasonal peak of close to 60 people fill out the ranks at the bistro, winery and vineyards.

"It's the employees that have grown with us that have made it possible for us to advance so quickly and well," said Curtis Bourgeois II, the eldest son. As manager, he continues to expand upon the foundation his father has built.

"I think Les Bourgeois is so successful because we've all worked so hard," said Dr. Bourgeois, "and because we entered the market at the same time this part of the country was demanding a drier California-type wine."

In addition to hard work and timing, family support has also played a vital role in the winery's success. Three of Curtis and Martha Bourgeois' four children fill important roles at the winery: Curtis Malcolm is the general manager, Karen is the office manager and Stephen is the architect who designed the new bistro.

A local newspaper's "Best of Boone County" contest deemed Les Bourgeois the best place to take out-of-town guests and the top place to buy wine. Responding to this kind of popularity, a few years ago the Bourgeois moved their winery from the A-frame on the bluffs to a larger location a mile away, just off the I-70 Rocheport Exit. Today, this building houses the Bourgeois' winemaking facilities, tasting room and gift shop.

Bourgeois family members from left to right are Martha, Curtis Malcolm, Curtis Horatio, Lucia, Stephen, Karen, Kristein and Ella.

During 1997, the winery expanded again by building a larger bluff-top wine garden and bistro. A long, winding walkway leads visitors to the 6,000-square-foot timber frame structure—crafted entirely from 80-year-old red and white Missouri oak. This new 150-seat bistro is just a mile north of I-70 on Route BB, beside their 6-acre vineyard. Here, Les Bourgeois' wines, made from native cultivars and French hybrid grapes, are complemented by fresh salads, soups and hearty provincial fare. (There's even Twinkies for the kids.)

Les Bourgeois is the perfect place to end a day of biking on the Katy Trail or antiquing in Rocheport. Chief winemaker Cory Bomgaars says Riverboat Red is the most popular wine and that the dry, white Vidal has won the most awards, including the American Wine Society's silver and the Florida State Fair's gold.

LES BOURGEOIS WINE LIST

Current Offerings:

BLUSH: A light, semi-dry wine. A delicate blend with subtle fruit tones.

JEUNETTE ROUGE: Fruity character and light body make this a refreshing, Northern Italian-style dry red. Composed of Chambourcin, Grenache and Cabernet.

LABELLE (formerly Vidal): A semi-dry German-style white with lush floral aromas and tropical fruit flavors, blended from Vidal and Muscat.

PINK FOX: Distinct grape flavors in this semi-sweet blush.

PREMIUM CLARET: A dry red with a deep color, spicy fruit aromas and earthy flavor of the Norton grape with a blend of Colorado Cabernet.

RIVERBOAT RED: A sweet red blend with fragrant fruit tones.

RIVERBOAT WHITE: A sweet white wine with honey and ripe melon flavors. This is a traditional Labrusca American-style wine.

SOLAY (formerly Seyval): A dry, crisp white with a citrus aroma. Made from Seyval, Vidal and Vignoles.

Les Bourgeois' winemakers: Cory Bomgaars (left) and Jeff Lynch.

Perhaps the only thing better than making wine for a living . . . playing with life-size Lincoln Logs. Here, Alan Judy (standing) and his crew, oversee the framing of the bistro. Six months of meticulous cutting were necessary to create the entirely wooden frame.

There's more than good food waiting for you at Les Bourgeois' new bistro. The architecture is as spellbinding as the river view just beyond the floor-to-ceiling windows. Exposed oak timbers, crafted by Heirloom Handcrafting of Macon, are the highlight of this building.

The bistro is one of the only modern-day examples of "authentic" timber framing used on such a large scale. There isn't a single nail in the entire substructure of this restaurant. Master timber framer Alan Judy used all-wood mortice and tenon connections, rather than metal bolts, to build the bistro's frame. Judy spent 6 months in his shop planing, cutting and finishing the timbers before the first beam was raised in May of 1996. This complex, zigzagged joinery is then further reinforced with wooden pegs.

And the tricks don't stop there. A ground source heat pump provides the heating and cooling. A 100-gallon-a-minute well uses the earth's cool underground temperatures to regulate the bistro's climate. Architect and son Stephen Bourgeois returned from Colorado to design and oversee this ambitious project.

As you admire the architecture, be sure to notice the chrome goose near the crown of the vaulted ceiling. It was crafted by Shawn Guerrero of Crested Butte, Colorado. The goose has long been the mascot of Les Bourgeois, but never before has the winery's logo been "reflected" in recycled chrome bumpers. I was told the chrome goose raised a bit of skepticism before alighting onto its permanent perch, but that once there, everyone said, "Oh, wow. It's perfect."

What started out as a weekend refuge put together piecemeal . . .

How the A-frame Came to "B"

by Jan Parenteau

In the late 1960s Ed and Hazel Williams were walking along the old Missouri Bluff Road when they found a perfect site for a cabin they had been thinking about building. It took a while, however, for Ed to persuade Gussie Nolte, the old bachelor who farmed the land to sell him 11 acres of it for a country home and garden.

What Ed had in mind was a far cry from the old 1850s traditional home at the corner of Second and Clark in Rocheport where his mother, Ada Williams, had lived for many years. Ed was intrigued with an interesting new design called an A-frame. He and Hazel thought it would be a perfect weekend home—a place to get away from the hustle and bustle of their busy city lives and perhaps someday they would be able to build their dream home a little closer to the road.

It was from the buildings being torn down on North Eighth in Columbia that Ed salvaged the materials he needed to build their cabin. The necessary 24-foot beams came from the basement of an old distributing company and the back door was from Cottle's Grocery. The plate glass for the front came from other buildings along Eighth. After the glass had been cut to his specifications Ed hauled it to the site very carefully on a boat trailer piled high with old mattresses.

"It was a wonderful retreat place," said Hazel Williams, "but at that time, it was also a place of scorpions and rattlesnakes and we had two small children. We also worried about the bluffs even though there was a fence." The fence was something they felt would soon be conquered by their inquisitive son, David.

They debated about selling the land, torn between letting go of their dream and an ever-increasing workload in Columbia. "We'll put a price on it so high no one will ever buy it," Ed said. It sold in a week!

Since that time, the A-frame has sheltered the family of Curtis and Martha Bourgeois while they built their home on the bluff. "Well . . . only for part of the family," said Curtis. "We had four children. The older three lived in a mobile home which we pulled to the site and the youngest child lived with us in the A-frame."

From 1983 to 1986, David Vaught and Shade Morris, both present residents of Rocheport, spent their bachelor years as roommates in the A-frame. "The bathroom facilities were a little tight," David said with a laugh. "We're talking about men well over six feet, a tiny tub and a sloping ceiling." The problem was resolved by an outside shower with hot and cold running water which served them faithfully year round.

Several people have owned this tiny home and land since Ed and Hazel parted with it. Curtis Bourgeois sold it once and then bought it back to house his new hobby, winemaking. Today, people from everywhere come to the A-frame and its surrounding garden picnic area to enjoy the ambiance provided by the magnificent view of the Missouri River and the many fine wines of one of Rocheport's most popular businesses, Les Bourgeois Winery & Vineyards.

From Rocheport Chronicles, *vol. 2, no. 4, fall 1994*

. . . has become one of mid-Missouri's most popular attractions.

EXPLORING STOVER
Buffalo Creek Vineyards & Winery

Eats • Parking • Post Office • Restrooms
Chamber of Commerce: (573) 377-2608

Stover is named after John Stover. In 1875 this retired colonel-turned-congressman succeeded in establishing a post office in western Morgan County. There was already a church, a school and several businesses.

As the Rock Island Line Railroad Company moved into the densely wooded area, the small village seemed poised for a bright future. But when the railroad was unable to get a few right-of-ways, it had to bypass the small village. Fortunately, the company soon decided to locate a depot with switching yards a few miles away, so Stover businesses simply relocated to be beside the economic vein. This new area was so heavily wooded that "Stumps" was briefly considered for the name of the new village. However in 1903 "Newstover" was recorded as the official name in the Morgan County court. Two years later the "New" was dropped.

In 1902 the young village was home to about 15 residents. The unpaved streets, with deep wagon ruts, were nearly impassable. Flourishing businesses included livery stables, a general store, a blacksmith and wagon-making shop and a saloon. In 1907, Stover's saloons closed for a four-year period when people in the county voted to make the sale of alcohol illegal. Stover's population today is around 1,000. Along with a few restaurants and gas stations, Stover has a number of quilt shops.

Bill Wooley and kids take a break in the shade with "Biff" and Jim Stephens.

BUFFALO CREEK
VINEYARDS & WINERY

Route 2, Box 65, Morgan County Road T-338, Stover, MO 65078
(573) 377-4535
Hours of Operation:
Monday through Saturday 10 a.m. to 6 p.m.
Sunday 11 a.m. to 6 p.m.

HOW TO GET THERE: Buffalo Creek Winery is located south of Stover, only half a mile from the Lake of the Ozarks. The winery is located southwest off Highway 135. Take Highway T to where the blacktop ends and then continue south (left), on County Road T-338. You'll be in densely wooded rolling hills. Just when you think you're lost, the gravel road opens up to the winery. Stop here for a visit, then continue on down the road to the new tasting room on the Lake of the Ozarks.

After his early retirement from electrical engineering in March 1988, James D. Stephens began what would become Buffalo Creek Vineyards & Winery. Fueled by his love of the outdoors and of good wine, he spent the next seven years starting a vineyard and building a winery. At first he just planted a few vines on half an acre. As these vines bore healthy fruit, he planted more and built trellises. For two years he sold his harvests to other wineries. Finally, in March 1995, he opened Buffalo Creek Vineyards & Winery.

Buffalo Creek is surrounded by almost a dozen acres of beautiful Ozark vineyard. There is a small tasting room and Stephens is happy to give tours to all his visitors.

By 1998, Stephens plans to expand his business considerably. He has purchased a larger piece of land closer to the lake and is converting a barn into a new winery and tasting room. From the deck outside the new place, Stephens says you can see for four miles both up and down the lake. There will also be a picnic area.

Stephens also plans to have a boat dock on the water, with a lift to take people to the new winery and back to their boats. The original tasting room and winery will remain open through this transition.

James is a self-taught vintner. He read various books and attended seminars put on by the state's Grape and Wine Advisory Program in Mountain Grove. Viticulture advisor Sanliang Gu helped him a lot along the way says Stephens, who refers to him warmly as "Guru Gu."

Hard work and patience have paid off at Buffalo Creek. In 1996, 1,200 gallons of several wines were produced, including Seyval, Vignoles, Concord, and Ruby Cabernet. Visitors should taste some of Buffalo Creek's Persimmon wine, which Stephens makes from the local wild persimmons.

Stephens says he'll have 11 acres in full production by 1999 and is planning to add some more every year. Other selections can be chosen in the tasting room before heading out to the picnic area to enjoy the sausage, cheese and crackers that are also available.

The tasting room at Buffalo Creek is secluded among
forested hills just a stone's throw away from Lake of the Ozarks.

Buffalo Creek is sort of an oasis far from other parts of Missouri's wine country. Bristle Ridge Winery, west of Sedalia, about 60 miles away, is his closest "competition."

"I would like to have more [wineries close by]," Stephens said. "It could happen soon . . . I think it'll happen. I think I'll be successful—and success breeds imitation."

BUFFALO CREEK WINE LIST

Current Offerings:
BUFFALO RED: A fruity, semi-dry red blend with a hint of oak.
CONCORD: A fruity, semi-dry red.
FOCH: A fruity, semi-dry red.
NATURAL PEAR: A fruity, semi-dry white with a hint of oak.
NATURAL PERSIMMON: A fruity, semi-dry white.
RUBY CABERNET: This heavy, dry red is oak-aged.
SEYVAL: A semi-dry, fruity varietal.
VIGNOLES: A fruity, semi-dry white wine.

Mark Geiger, a Columbia resident and professor at William Woods University, inspects the remains of an old cellar at the Boonville Wine Company. Geiger's great-great-great-grandfather William Haas established the winery, which closed in 1874.

History Section:
A LOOK BACK IN BOONVILLE

by Sara Ervanian

If Mark Geiger could have his way, he would reclaim the land that his great-great-great-grandfather owned here and replant the family crop: Catawba grapes. Then, the mild-mannered business professor from Columbia would make wine just like his ancestor, vintner William Haas, did at Boonville Wine Company on the banks of the Missouri River in Boonville shortly before the Civil War.

At that time, grapes were the biggest-paying cash crop in Missouri, Geiger said, better even than tobacco or hemp. Haas was selling his Catawba wine for between $2 and $2.50 a gallon, or about double the price of wine made by his fellow vintners downriver in Hermann.

The German immigrant also brewed beer in his 80-square-foot stone brewery built on the hills west of town, on privately owned land not far from what is known today as Harley Park. The brewery closed in 1874 and never reopened. Geiger would like a chance to sample a bit of his past.

"That's my pipe dream," Geiger said with an air of reverie. "To buy back the land and plant a vine or two."

Since January, Geiger has been combing through old newspaper articles, circuit court cases, land transfers, military records and epitaphs to piece together a profile of Haas, his business and his family, which included a wife, Marie, and nine children. So far, Geiger has managed to extract an extraordinary amount of information despite the fact that he's never uncovered a photograph of his ancestor, nor has he found a surviving wine bottle, label or logo from the winery/brewery. "The Haases are as vanished as the Sumerians," Geiger said.

What Geiger has managed to uncover about Haas paints a picture of an industrious, energetic and intelligent man born to working-class parents in 1800 in Halwitzheim, Germany. The family emigrated to the United States in 1830 and settled in Watertown, N.Y. Three years later, Geiger said, Haas founded the first brewery in Chicago when the town was still a village with a population of 150. The brewery grew to become the largest in Chicago before the Civil War. It burned in the Great Fire of 1871 and was never rebuilt.

In 1840, however, Haas sold his interest in the Chicago brewery, Geiger said, and moved to St. Louis. In 1846, he moved to Boonville and bought 7.92 acres of land for a brewery. Beer was brewed at the site the first year and wine production began in 1849, Geiger said. The four-story brewery included two levels above ground (the pressroom and sleeping rooms for the workers) and two levels below ground (a fermenting room and six wine cellars).

Today, the remains of the stone brewery resemble the ruins of a forgotten castle tangled in the brush and trees, invisible from the nearby railroad tracks. At its height, Geiger said, the Boonville Wine Company encompassed 115 acres, including Harley Park.

Haas died in 1862, which was the first in a series of circumstances—the Civil War, a collapsing Missouri wine industry, grapes that were vulnerable to disease and heirs unsuited to carry on the family business—that led to the closing of the company 12 years later. "It was all very unfortunate," Geiger said.

Boonville folk singer and historian Bob Dyer would like to see the brewery ruins preserved as a state historic site. "To me," he said, "the ruins are an important and significant site in the history of the state, not just Boonville."

Reprinted from the Columbia Daily Tribune, *August 22, 1994*

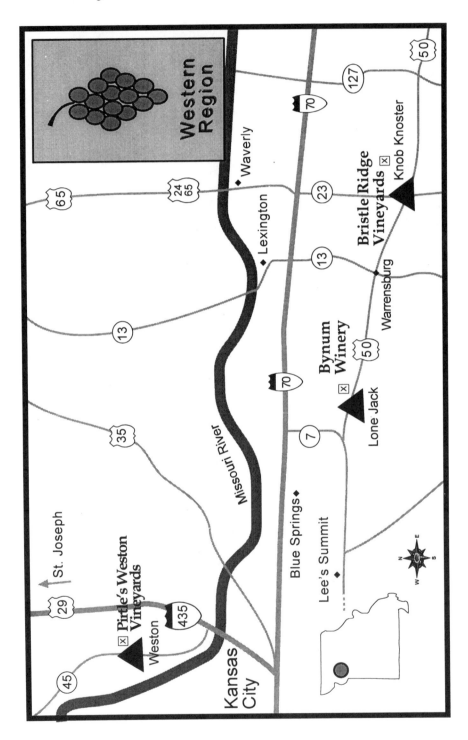

WESTERN REGION

Cattle herds and corn rows are associated with western Missouri agriculture more than grape vines—but vineyards are out here, too. In the coming years there could soon be as many as five wineries around Kansas City and along Highway 50. Currently there are three, highlighted in the next few pages.

Just outside Knob Knoster in Montserrat, Bristle Ridge Vineyards & Winery has one of the oldest vineyards in production in the state, and one of the most scenic, rural settings you can find. Bynum Winery is newer to the scene and offers a different feel, along with some good wine. And Pirtle's Weston Vineyards, just north of Kansas City, has all the historic atmosphere of a Missouri river town.

EXPLORING KNOB NOSTER
Bristle Ridge Vineyards & Winery

Eats • Gas • Lodging • Parking • Post Office • Restrooms
Knob Noster Chamber of Commerce: (816) 563-2444

The town of Knob Noster lies 70 miles east of Kansas City on Highway 50. Knob Noster is home to Whiteman Air Force Base, named to honor pilot and 2nd Lieut. George Whiteman, a Sedalia native, who was killed during the Japanese attack on Pearl Harbor.

This base is home to 13 B-2 Spirit bombers, otherwise known as Stealth Bombers. It is not entirely uncommon to see these sleek black crafts sliding silently through the air. In fact, with their jagged wingspan stretching 172 feet and a cabin height of only 17 feet, this plane looks more like a UFO than an aircraft (and I should know). This sleek design helps the craft evade enemy radar.

The Air Force press release explains it best. "The B-2's low observability is derived from reduced infrared, acoustic, electromagnetic, visual and radar signatures. These signatures make it difficult for the sophisticated defensive systems to detect, track and engage the B-2." If you've gotta have one, raid your penny jar and bring an extra $1.3 billion along—and it only comes in black.

Whiteman Air Force Base is also responsible for the vast network of now defunct Minuteman II missile silos and launch control centers spread out over 5,300 square miles of central Missouri. These products of the Cold War, completed in 1964, are now being "imploded," according to the Public Affairs office.

Back at the base, there is a museum of the Launch Control Facility for the ICBM. "Spirit" tours can be arranged (in advance only) by calling (816) 687-6123.

Not far from the Air Force base, along State Road 132, lies Knob Noster State Park. This beautiful park is full of silver maples, burr oaks, pin oaks and white oaks, along with a buttonbush shrub swamp. The park is perfect for camping, fishing, horseback riding, hiking and mountain biking. It is also equipped with restrooms, showers and laundry facilities. A nominal fee is charged for camping. Also part of the park is the Royal Oaks Golf Course, a public course managed by Whiteman Air Force Base.

So where did the name Knob Noster come from? Upon its founding in 1846, Knob Noster took its name from two prominent mounds on a nearby prairie. Noster in Latin means "our," so the translation is "our mounds." Shortly after its founding, the town moved closer to the newly completed Missouri Pacific Railroad. Only one year after the move, the wooden buildings on Main Street burned to the ground. These buildings were replaced, constructed from locally produced bricks.

The knobs are an important landmark and are the subject of several interesting legends. Some locals tell of a great battle between two Native American tribes, after which, the mounds were erected as a burial monument for those slain in the battle. Another legend tells of lost Native American treasures buried in the mounds. Several treasure hunters have tried their luck digging in the mounds but most have met with little success. One group of treasure hunters did manage to make an interesting find. They uncovered several human skeletons and a variety of artifacts from an early mound-dwelling tribe.

Motels
Whiteman Inn
(816) 563-3000

Bell Towers
(816) 563-3044

Restaurants
Gourmet Buffet
(816) 563-6748

Leo's
(816) 563-3113

Looking down
the rows at Bristle Ridge
Vineyards & Winery.

BRISTLE RIDGE
VINEYARDS & WINERY

P.O. Box 95, Knob Noster, MO 65336
(816) 229-0961
Hours of Operation:
Saturday 10 a.m. to 5 p.m.
Sunday 11 a.m. to 5 p.m.

HOW TO GET THERE: From Sedalia go west on US 50, past Knob Noster. Bristle Ridge is located about 2 miles outside town in Montserrat. At Montserrat follow the signs a half mile south to the winery. You can also take US 50 from Kansas City. Look for the signs at Montserrat about 4 miles east of Warrensburg.

Bristle Ridge Vineyards & Winery is a small family-owned winery that produces a wide variety of French hybrid wines. With their large variety of wines, you will undoubtedly find something to please your palate.

Their wines range in sweetness from subtle dry whites to bright sweet reds. In the fall they also make hard cider—a perfect treat for cold winter nights.

A three-story building that originally served as a water tower in the 1950s now houses the winery and tasting room. Bristle Ridge's panoramic hilltop view, which once served as a lookout for Civil War soldiers, is a great spot for an afternoon picnic. Breads, cheeses and summer sausage can also be purchased at the winery.

Be sure and bring the kids along to enjoy some of the Bristle Ridge grape juice. Next to the winery is an orchard, soon to become Montserrat Vineyards, where you can still purchase several types of fresh fruit when in season.

BRISTLE RIDGE WINE LIST
Current Offerings:

BURGUNDY	SAUTERNE
DECHAUNCE	SEYVAL BLANC
DIAMOND	SOLÉ BLANC
HARD CIDER	VIDAL BLANC
MONT ROSÉ	VILLARD BLANC
MONTSERRAT RED	VILLARD NOIR

EXPLORING LONE JACK
Bynum Winery

Eats • Parking • Museum • Post Office • Powell Gardens • Restrooms
Lone Jack Civil War Museum (816) 566-2272
City Hall (816) 697-2503

Upon its founding in the mid-1840s, Lone Jack was named for a single blackjack tree, which marked the location of a spring on the prairie site. A marble monument in town marks where Confederate and Union forces engaged in some of the fiercest hand-to-hand combat of the Civil War. The Lone Jack Civil War Museum documents this battle and several others that occurred in the area. About 500 people live in Lone Jack today, and it's growing fast as people from Kansas City and Lee's Summit move out to the country.

Martin Rice was a poet laureate
from Jackson County.
His poems deal with many issues,
including Civil War battles
he witnessed.

Here's a stanza from his poem,
"The Cruel War Is Over."

'Tis done—
the bloody strife is over,
the storm of war has passed—
We hear the marching tramp
no more,
of men in armor massed.

From *Rural Rhymes & Talks*
& Tales of Olden Times, 1904

Floyd Bynum

BYNUM WINERY

13520 S. Sam Moore Road, Lone Jack, MO 64070

(816) 566-2240

Hours of Operation:

Open seven days a week, noon to 5:30 p.m.

Mondays and Wednesdays noon to 4 p.m.

HOW TO GET THERE: From I-70, east of Kansas City, head south at Exit 28, Oak Grove, on Route F. At 50 Highway go left a short bit. Then make a right onto Sam Moore Road.

With a background in food chemistry, winemaking and vineyard operation, Floyd Bynum has developed the unique wines of the Bynum Winery. His wines are made from Seyval Blanc, Villard Blanc and Chancellor Noir grapes. Bynum also produces fruit wines from cherries, apples and other fruits. Bynum produces at least 1,000 gallons of these wines annually.

Bynum starts his plants from seed, something most vineyards don't do. He says he can buy 1,000 seeds for the cost of one healthy young plant.

The first Bynums were Europeans who settled in the Lone Jack area. Floyd Bynum's great-grandmother was a Native American who married a Bynum and stayed behind when the rest of her tribe were forced out of their homeland and relocated to South Dakota. Bynum's great uncle, George Shawhan, was famous for producing Shawhan Whiskey before Prohibition.

When you visit the winery you may meet Mr. Bynum himself while trying his selection of fine wines. When you're actually able to meet the maker of the wine you're about to taste for the first time, it adds an intimacy to the experience. This is part of the charm of visiting the smaller wineries. At the winery you will also find several unique gifts including a large selection of Watkin's Spices and a wealth of crafts made by a local artist.

Nearby: Powell Gardens is four miles east of Bynum Winery. The garden is open year-round and is the perfect complement to a trip to Bynum Winery.

BYNUM WINE LIST

Current Offerings:

APPLE WINE: Available in sweet or semi-dry, delicate finish of smooth, ripe apples.
BACO NOIR: Dry, aged, smooth, dark as ink and rich in flavor.
CHANCELLOR NOIR: Dry, Bordeaux-style wine with intense flavor, crimson color.
CONCORD: An old-time favorite.
FOXY RED: Semi-dry, light Bordeaux-style wine with a beautiful color.
MISS MEADOW LARK: Semi-dry, with hints of oak and vanilla.
RED TAIL: Dry, Bordeaux-style, top of the line, intense flavor and color.
SEYVAL BLANC: Dry, cool, crisp oak and vanilla flavor.
VIDAL BLANC: Semi-dry, cool, crisp and fruity flavor.
VIGNOLE BLANC: Dry, smooth finish, full-bodied wine.
VILLARD BLANC: Available in sweet or dry, crisp, smooth flavor.
WHITE DOVE: Sweet, smooth flavor, delicate palate with hints of oak and vanilla.

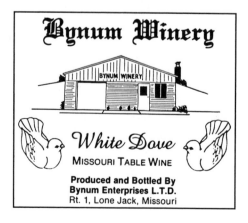

Bynum Winery

BYNUM WINERY

White Dove
MISSOURI TABLE WINE

Produced and Bottled By
Bynum Enterprises L.T.D.
Rt. 1, Lone Jack, Missouri

Visit a wee bit o' Ireland in Weston. Bob Reeder, an Irish folk musician, has been taking audiences "back to the homeland" for ten years at O'Malley's 1842 Irish Pub. Be sure and visit on Sundays, when he plays from 3 to 9 p.m. This classic Irish pub is tucked down in the cellars of the American Bowman Restaurant at the corner of Short and Welt Streets.

EXPLORING WESTON

Pirtle's Weston Vineyards

Antiques • Restaurants • Eats • B & Bs • Post Office • Museum
Weston Information Center: (816) 640-2909

Located just 20 minutes north of Kansas City on Highway 45, Weston is a great little town that has retained many of its historic homes and buildings. In the 1800s Weston was an important port of call along the Missouri River, until the river changed course and left the town landlocked.

The town was founded in 1837, after 2 million acres of Missouri's northwest corner was opened to pioneer settlement by the Platte Purchase. Weston quickly grew to become the second largest port in Missouri, as its population surged to around 5,000 citizens.

In addition to its river access, Weston was also an important departure point for wagon trains headed west. Steamboats would arrive at the port loaded with pioneers ready to venture into the western territories. They would leave stocked with locally grown tobacco and hemp to trade farther out West.

Even today, huge tobacco barns still in use dot the rolling hills as Highway 45 takes you past large farms and stately country mansions. It's easy to distinguish a tobacco barn from a hay barn by the thin vertical vents or windows that often stretch several stories high. These special windows help regulate the speed of the tobacco-drying process.

Hemp and tobacco supported Weston's economy during its heyday as a river town. They remained successful crops until the 1857 flood took the meandering Missouri River elsewhere. Without its river access, the town's economy suffered. The population shrank nearly as fast as had risen only 20 years before.

The town remained practically untouched for nearly 100 years. Many of the aging buildings and homes have now been restored and the business district is rising again to its previous grandeur. In 1972, Weston was designated a Historic District and placed on the National Register of Historic Places.

Today, Weston's business district supports a healthy tourist business with stores like The Town Mouse and Plum Pudding. Weston is also home to Snow Creek ski area, a winery and many museums. The town of 1,440 is dotted with several pre–Civil War homes and a good selection of bed & breakfasts. If you enjoy exploring the rolling countryside and quiet, lovingly restored towns, Weston is for you.

McCormack's Distillery is also nearby. Founded in 1856, this business is the oldest producer of bourbon west of the Mississippi. The Weston Historical Museum is also highly recommended. Their number is (816) 386-2977.

Bed & Breakfasts

Benner House
(816) 640-2616

The Inn at Weston Landing
(816) 640-5788

The Hatchery
(816) 640-5700

The Lemon Tree
(816) 386-5367

Apple Creek Inn
(816) 640-5724

Annual Events

February: Heritage Days
March: Antique Show and Sale
April: Annual Antique & Collectible Flea Market
May: Bed & Breakfast Homes Tour
June: Music in the Park, Citywide Garage Sale, Wheels to Weston
July: Music in the Park, Weston Jaycees Annual July 4th Celebration, Kids Day
August: Weston Summer Glow
September: Classic Car Show
October: Applefest
December: Christmas in Weston Homes Tour

Pirtle's is housed in an old church building, seen here in the window reflection of The Vineyards Restaurant, across the street. If you're looking for a cozy dining spot, this is it.

PIRTLE'S WESTON VINEYARDS

502 Spring Street, Weston, MO 64098
(816) 640-5728 or (816) 386-5200
Hours of Operation:
Monday through Saturday 10 a.m. to 6p.m.
Sunday 11 a.m. to 6 p.m.

HOW TO GET THERE: Located in downtown Weston, about 20 miles northwest of Kansas City off I-29 or I-435 north.

The winery and cellars at Pirtle's Weston Vineyards are housed in a restored German Lutheran Evangelical church constructed in the 1860s. The French hybrid grape varieties that produce the Pirtle wines are grown in the 13-acre Pirtle vineyard in Camden Point. Varieties include Villard Noir and Leon Millot. Along with their fine grape varietals, the vintner and owner Elber

Pirtle also makes wonderful apple wine from apples grown in local orchards. Platte County is famous for its apple production, and Pirtle's apple wine is sure to please. Pirtle also produces mead, also called honey wine. Mead was one of the first wines ever produced, reportedly being enjoyed long before grapes were even being cultivated.

The word "honeymoon" originated from an English tradition involving mead. Mead was considered a love potion so, according to tradition, newlyweds were to drink mead from "moon to moon" (one month). Mead is a great after-dinner wine. With some cheese and fruit it makes an appetizing combination. Mead is moderately sweet and should be served chilled.

Pirtle's Winery also sells replicas of the hand-blown glass goblets used for drinking mead throughout the Viking and Celtic regions of Northern Europe. This was a time when even your most right-hand Norseman could try to poison you, so the glasses have no base, which prevents you from putting the goblet down before your cup is empty.

According to Jim French, author of *Meads, Maids and Mayhem,* the original goblet was found in Birka, Sweden, the Viking's major trading post to the East, and is believed to date from the 7th century.

Be sure and visit Pirtle's newly opened wine garden where you can relax and enjoy a bottle of Pirtle wine while munching on some sausage, cheese, Tuscan loaves and fruit.

PIRTLE'S WINE LIST

Current Offerings:

APPLE WINE: Made from Missouri apples, fermented in whiskey barrels.

MEAD: Sweet dessert wine. Winner of the bronze medal at the Pacific Rim International Wine Competition and a gold medal at the Indiana State Fair.

MELLOW RED: A soft fruity red with lots of great flavor and aroma. Bronze medal, Indiana State Fair.

RASPBERRY MEAD: Made from 94 percent honey and 6 percent raspberries in a blush wine style. Silver Medal, Indiana State Fair.

SPARKLING MEAD: This mead has earned numerous awards, including gold medal at the Indiana State Fair; gold medal at the Pacific Rim International Wine Competition; and the bronze medal at the Louisiana County Fair.

WESTON BEND RED: Premium dry red table wine made from Chambourcin grapes, matured in oak. Winner of silver and bronze medals.

WESTON BEND WHITE: Semi-sweet white wine.

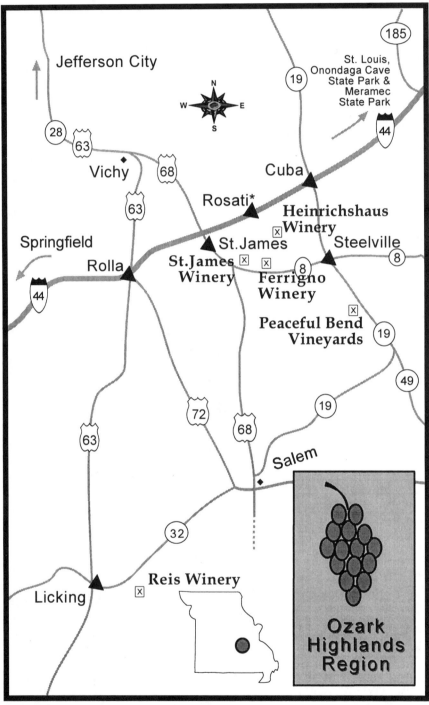

*Rosati Winery Outlet

OZARK HIGHLANDS REGION

The Ozark Highlands region has a long winemaking tradition. By the 1870s, there were vineyards in nearby Rolla and Dillon. Italian immigrants settled in the St. James area and planted their own vineyards. By 1922, there were 200 vineyards in the region with more than 2,000 acres in production.

Many vineyards were under contract with Welch's grape juice operation located nearby in Arkansas. When these contracts came to an end, many vineyards went out of business, and others began growing grape varieties more suited for winemaking.

Buying grapes from roadside stands is still a tradition here, and it's hard to get lost on these rolling country roads without seeing several magnificent vineyards. Be sure and leave plenty of time for exploring Maramec Spring Park, too.

EXPLORING ST. JAMES

Ferrigno Vineyards & Winery, Heinrichshaus Vineyard & Winery, St. James Winery

B & Bs • City Park • Eats • Lodging • Parking • Post Office • Restrooms
Tourist Information Center: (573) 265-3899

Sitting in the middle of perfect soil and weather for growing grapes the Ozark Highlands region was designated an official viticultural area in 1987.

The St. James area was first settled in 1826 when an Ohio banker sent Samuel Massey to the area in search of minerals. Massey found enough iron ore to start the Maramec Iron Works at the site of the Maramec Spring. Land was soon purchased along the prairie nearby to start a settlement that was initially called Jamestown. However, once the locals learned that another Jamestown already existed in Missouri, they changed their name to St. James.

In the early years the iron was shipped by river and used to make cooking utensils and farming implements. Later, when the railroad came to town, St. James continued to grow as the demand for iron ore increased. By 1876, however, production slowed and the works closed shortly thereafter.

Today, the remains of the iron works and the 1857 cold-blast furnace stand like forgotten ruins in the jungles of Central America. The ruins are preserved right next to Maramec Spring in Maramec Spring Park, located 6 miles south of town on Highway 8. In addition to the spring and the iron works, this beautiful park is great for trout fishing, camping and hiking. There are also two museums. For more information call Maramec Spring Park at (573) 265-7387.

While in St. James, you'll find shops and eateries throughout town, especially along West Springfield and North Jefferson Streets. The newest restaurant is the highly recommended Douglas Company.

Just 12 miles west on I-44 lies Rolla, home of the University of Missouri–Rolla along with several fine restaurants, shops and taverns that make the St. James area not only the perfect daytrip destination, but a great vacation spot.

Just north of St. James on Highway 63, there's a great road to explore. It's located directly across from a pull-off with a "Scenic Overlook" sign. A "Road closed 6 miles ahead" sign on the east side of the road marks your arrival. Highlights include a the Vichy fire tower, an old cemetery, Spring Gap Conservation Area with hiking trails and primitive camping and some gorgeous views. The road dead-ends right before the Gasconade River.

Bed & Breakfasts
The Painted Lady
(573) 265-5008
Note: Both Ferrigno Vineyards & Winery and
Rosati Wine Outlet also operate B & Bs.

Visit Maramec Spring Park to feed the trout (above), and explore the 1857 cold-blast furnace (left). Other nearby highlights include hiking trails, state parks and the Vichy fire tower (far right).

Annual Events

May: Wine Festival, Strawberry Festival
June: Wine Expo
July: Route 66 Summerfest
August: Grape Fall Festival & Parade, Street Market & Craft Sale, Antique Show
September: Fall Bicycle Tour
October: Old Iron Works Days and German Oktoberfest
December: Christmas City of the Ozarks

St. James Winery is a family business, run by Pat Hofherr
and her three sons, including son Peter, shown above.

ST. JAMES WINERY

540 Sidney Street, St. James, MO 65559
(573) 265-7912 or 1 (800) 280-WINE
Hours of Operation:
Monday through Saturday 8 a.m. to 7 p.m.
Sunday 11 a.m. to 7 p.m. Closes at 6 p.m. in winter

HOW TO GET THERE: Take I-44 to St. James. Head north on Highway 68 and take
the first right onto Route B (the north service road of I-44). Follow Route B for half
a mile to the winery. The winery is easily visible from I-44.

In 1970, James Hofherr and his wife, Pat, started their winery in the
Ozark foothills outside St. James. Mr. Hofherr had worked as a brewmaster
for the Falstaff Brewery and as a winemaker for Bardenheier's Wine Cellars and
Post Winery. The family tradition lives on today as Pat and her three sons, An-
drew, John and Peter, run one of the most technologically advanced wineries in the
state. They have become one of the most nationally and internationally awarded
wineries in the state.

In 1995 alone, the Hofherrs won more than 75 awards in local, national and
international wine competitions. A national magazine named their 1993 Seyval one
of the top 50 wines in the world.

"Our '93 Norton has even won best red wine at an international competition," Peter said. "There are only 3 to 4 Missouri wineries in history that have won this honor."

When you visit the St. James Winery you can sample the excellence of their wines for yourself. You might also like to visit their large gift shop, which features gourmet edibles, souvenirs, wine-related books and a large selection of home winemaking supplies. The staff is happy to let you taste from their wide variety of wines, or show you the facility while answering any questions you might have.

The St. James wines are produced from vineyards nearby. The Native American and French hybrid grapes used to make the St. James wines all grow well in this prime area. The winery produces upwards of 20,000 cases of wine per year, and they are continually planting new vineyards to keep up with the growing demand for their wines. The crew manages 80 acres of vineyards and is working on adding another 20 acres.

ST. JAMES WINE LIST

Current Offerings:
BARREL FERMENTED SEYVAL: A full-bodied, dry varietal white wine that has complex oak tones produced by fermenting in new French oak barrels.
BLACKBERRY: A sweet berry wine made from 100 percent blackberry juice.
CABERNET SAUVIGNON: A dry red made from Napa valley grapes.
CHAMPAGNE: A French-style Brut aged on the yeast. A gold medal winner.
CONCORD GRAPE JUICE: A naturally sweet juice made from Concord grapes with no added water or preservatives.
COUNTRY RED: A full-bodied semi-dry red blend of American and French hybrid. A gold medal winner.
COUNTRY WHITE: A semi-dry, cold-fermented Catawba.
DRY VIGNOLES: Dry white with intense citrus qualities.
JOHANNISBERG REISLING: A German-style, cold-fermented wine.
LATE HARVEST SEYVAL '95: A delicious sweet wine with 17 percent residual sugar.
NORTON: A dry wine aged in American and Hungarian oak. Winner of nine gold medals.
NOUVEAU: A semi-dry red, juicy with a cherry nose.
PINK CATAWBA: Sweet Catawba blush. Winner of five medals in 1996.
PRIVATE RESERVE CABERNET SAUVIGNON '93: A rich, full-bodied red made from California grapes.
SCHOOL HOUSE BLUSH: 2 percent natural residual sugar.
SCHOOL HOUSE RED: A fruity, light-bodied, dry red blend from Missouri grapes.
SCHOOL HOUSE WHITE: A Riesling-style wine made from Delaware grapes. 2.5 percent residual sugar. Winner of a double gold at the San Diego Wine Fair.
SEYVAL BLANC: Possesses a distinctive Seyval character with 2 percent natural sugar. Winner of the gold medal at the Missouri State Fair.
SPARKLING BLUSH: A fully balanced sparkling wine. Silver medal winner at the Missouri State Fair.
SPARKLING NIAGARA: A sparkling Niagara juice. Naturally sweet.
VELVET RED: A sweet Concord. Gold medal winner at the Riverside California Fair and at the Florida State wine competitions.
VELVET WHITE: A sweet Niagara. Gold medal winner at the Riverside California Fair.
VIGNOLES: Vintage '94 with 3 percent natural sugar. Winner of two gold medals.
VINTNER'S RESERVE SEYVAL '95: A semi-dry white wine full of tropical fruit flavors. Gold medal winner.

FERRIGNO VINEYARDS & WINERY

17301 State Route B, St. James, MO 65559

(573) 265-7742 or (573) 265-8050

Hours of Operation:

Monday through Saturday 10 a.m. to 6 p.m

Sunday noon to 6 p.m.

Weekends only during January, February and March.

HOW TO GET THERE: Take I-44 to St. James. Turn north on Highway 68 and take the first right onto Route B (the north I-44 service road). After passing St. James Winery, follow Route B for just over 4 miles. The winery will be on your left.

The rustic scenery and fine wines of the Ferrigno Winery (pronounced Fur-EEN-yo) exemplify the romance and flavor of Missouri wine country. The winery and tasting room are housed in an old dairy barn surrounded by several acres of beautiful vineyard. With its covering of well-weathered wood and a welcome sign mingled among the antiques near the entrance, the barn welcomes you with an atmosphere of warmth and hospitality.

The winery's covered deck offers a view of the vineyard to the west. This is the perfect place to enjoy a relaxing afternoon with friends or a romantic sunset with someone special.

The handcrafted wines of the Ferrigno Winery are made entirely from Missouri-grown grapes. The entire process, from crushing grapes to aging the wines is done on the Ferrigno estate. All of Ferrigno's wines are aged in stainless steel tanks with the exception of the dry red wines, which are aged in barrels made of Missouri white oak. The majority of the wines are sold directly from the winery. Dick and Susan Ferrigno have one goal that guides their winemaking: "to produce clean, flavorful wines of premium quality and distinctive regional character."

Dick Ferrigno is a gracious host who works hard to make his winery a special place to visit. The winery is open for private dinners, wine tastings and receptions in its heated wine garden room. You might also like to prepare a picnic from the deli or browse the wine-related gifts that line the tasting room. You can even turn your visit into a memorable overnight stay at Ferrigno's Bed & Breakfast. A stay in the guesthouse or in the private loft above the winery is accompanied by complimentary wine and breakfast.

FERRIGNO WINE LIST

Current Offerings:

CHAMBOURCIN RED: Dry, oak-aged red varietal with medium body, deep color, rich fruit flavors and a spicy nose.

CONCORD: A classic, sweet, dessert-style red wine.

GARDEN BLUSH: Semi-sweet rosé. Light with a wild grape flavor.

GARDEN RED: Light, semi-sweet red.

GOLDEN HARVEST: A sweet white wine.

PRIMAVERA: Semi-dry with a zesty spring-time flavor and a hint of sweetness. Floral and spice overtones of the Missouri Riesling grape.

SEYVAL: Semi-dry varietal. Clean and pleasantly tart, with a delicate fruit flavor.

VINO DI FAMIGLIA: Semi-dry red blend with a mellow fruitiness.

Here, Dick "thiefs" a sampling of an aging red wine from an oak barrel.

HEINRICHSHAUS
VINEYARD & WINERY

18500 State Route U, Saint James MO 65559
(573)265-5000
Hours of Operation:
Monday through Saturday 9 a.m. to 6 p.m.
Sunday noon to 6 p.m., closed Wednesday

HOW TO GET THERE: To visit Heinrichshaus Vineyard and Winery take I-44 to Highway 68 at St. James. Follow Route KK 4 miles to Route U. Go north on U for 3 miles and look for the entrance to the winery.

Founded on the belief that affordable, high-quality wine can be produced in Missouri, The Heinrichshaus Vineyard & Winery has been producing wine since 1978.

Instead of adding specialized laboratory yeast to his wines, winemaker and owner Heinrich Grohe uses the natural bloom of yeast that grows on the grape. Heinrich uses his well-developed skills to determine when a wine is ready for drinking and in what fashion it will be presented. Each wine is treated as an individual. Each offering is tested and tasted to determine which aging method best suits its character. No sugar is added during the winemaking process. A varietal wine that might have been dry one year might be semi-sweet the next, depending on the weather conditions when the grapes were grown.

Nearly all of the Heinrichshaus wines are made from French hybrid and Native American grape varieties. The Heinrichshaus wines have won many gold, silver and best-of-show medals. Heinrich's specialty is dry wine but you may find a semi-sweet or semi-dry to suit your tastes. You might also try one of Heinrich's experimental which wines are available from time to time.

When Heinrich emigrated to the United States from Germany in the 1950s he found Missouri wines to be quite different from those he knew in Europe. In order to find a wine that he could enjoy with his meals, Heinrich began experimenting with Missouri grapes. After honing his skills with the native grapes, Heinrich and his family purchased a tract of land and began planting the Heinrichshaus Vineyard. In the early years of grape production he sold his grapes to other wineries, but all the while plans for the Heinrichshaus Winery were in the works. Construction began in 1978 and one year later the doors of the winery were opened to the public.

When you visit Heinrichshaus you will likely get a chance to meet Heinrich himself. If a relaxing picnic sounds good, head to the terrace where you can spend a carefree afternoon in the shade while nibbling on sausage and cheeses.

HEINRICHSHAUS WINE LIST

Current Offerings:

CHAMBOURCIN
CYNTHIANA
PRAIRIE BLANC
PRAIRIE GOLD
PRAIRIE ROSE

PRAIRIE ROUGHE
VIDAL '93
VIDAL BLANC '92
VIGNOLES

vintage 1994

HEINRICHSHAUS

Phelps County
CYNTHIANA

*A full-bodied dry red table wine
made from the Cynthiana grape,
grown in the Ozark Highlands of Missouri
Christina Lorraine Vineyard*

Produced and bottled by HEINRICHSHAUS VINEYARDS and WINERY
St. James, Missouri 65559 — Missouri Bonded Winery 107

Historical Essay:
THE STARK STAR SHINES AGAIN
by Phyllis Meagher

"Dear Sir: We beg to call your attention
to a most promising new Grape we have secured . . ."

So began a letter written January 9, 1902, by William Stark, treasurer of Stark Brothers' Nurseries & Orchards Co. of Louisiana, Mo. "We will invest a great deal of money in this variety," he continued, "which may be called Stark for the present. . . . Certainly no grape is more beautiful and attractive."

The path that led me to Mr. Stark's letter began with a neighborly comment not long after I bought my 15-acre Concord vineyard in St. James.

"That last row isn't Concord," said Lou Tessaro. "It's the late grape. You'd better let me prune it. You can't let as many buds as with Concord or you'll overload it."

He was right. The late grape was different. (Lou was always right, I learned, and not just about grapes—there would be many more Lou lessons for this neophyte country dweller.) It bloomed later, produced big, shouldered bunches and ripened a good month after the Concords were off the vines.

The late grape was also susceptible to black rot, and it seemed to push new growth from everywhere, even mid-trunk. Suckering was serious business with that row. And, true to folklore, we harvested that row after the first frost.

My curiosity aroused, I questioned my elderly neighbor Mr. Stoltz, who had over 100 acres of grapes, including some 20 varieties. "The late grape is the Stark Star," he said. He thought it had been developed by one of the old grape experimenters of the last century, maybe Munson.

A call to Roy Renfro of the Munson Memorial Vineyard in Dennison, Texas, ruled out that possibility. But some additional sleuthing turned up historical records about the Stark Star grape. Louis Zellner of Granby, Mo., reported in the 1904 report of the State Horticultural Society of Missouri that the Stark Star "ripens about the 1st of October, but does not fully mature until frost has stripped the leaves from the vines."

That sounded familiar. By now, I was fairly sure of two things. My grapes were the Stark Star, and I was hooked on Missouri grape history.

Missouri history is resplendent with grapes. Then, as now, grapes fascinated, intrigued, puzzled and excited Missourians. At the turn of the century, nearly everyone was trying to find suitable varieties for eating and winemaking that grow well in our climate.

Varieties were cross-bred, sent to experimental stations and nurseries, set up in commercial plots with "successful and responsible vineyardists," planted and observed by professional and amateurs alike.

Mr. Stark's attention-getting letter was well received. The Stark Star was sent as far away as the Geneva Experimental Station in New York, where written logs still exist of bloom, growing conditions and harvest dates for the next 17 years.

Some varieties, either because of their inability to flourish in our climate or because of their uninteresting wine and juice qualities, passed from current interest. Others didn't survive the Volstead Act. Sometimes, even in places like my vineyard where old varieties were tended, their histories were lost . . . or almost.

The Stark Star trail, which led from Missouri to Arkansas and back to Missouri, started with Professor Joseph Bachman, an immigrant from Lucerne, Switzerland, who settled in Altus, Arkansas, in 1881. He was eulogized in the *American Fruit Grower Magazine* in 1928 as "one of the most expert grape culturists in the U.S." The grape that was to become the Stark Star was one of Professor Bachman's first successes. He crossed the Cynthiana (also called Norton's Virginia Seedling) and Catawba and won a silver medal with the grape at the St. Louis Exposition in 1904. He then sold the rights to the grape to Stark Brothers' Nursery, who introduced it commercially.

While both its parents are still familiar to today's consumers of Missouri wine and juice, the Stark Star made a brief, brilliant flash on the scene and then disappeared. But, like a comet, the Stark Star reappears every so often to take a bow.

Its first reappearance in our time was as a dessert wine and then a port, produced by Lucian Dressel of Mount Pleasant Winery in Augusta after he discovered this new/old grape in St. James.

The fall of 1994 was the first crush at Adam Puchta Winery. I delivered a load of Stark Stars to the winery on a crisp, sunny afternoon in October. There's something to be said for the Stark Star's late ripening. Picking on a nice, cool October day is a delightful reward for making it through our hot August harvest.

It was the sort of mid-October harvest day that inspired Mark Twain to say that to be in Missouri in October is to know heaven. Handling crush along with their first Octoberfest crowds was a little tricky for winemaker Tim Puchta and his wife, Vicki. At small wineries like theirs, the salesroom staff and the cellar rats are one and the same. We all pitched in to crush the grapes while Spencer, the seventh generation Puchta, observed from his stroller.

The grapes were beautiful, dark blue, almost black. Juice was pumped from the crusher and de-stemmer on the patio to a jacketed stainless steel tank in the arched stone cellars. This was an experimental batch of only a few hundred pounds of grapes, so crushing didn't take long. Clean-up, on the other hand, did.

Tim is a fanatic about cleanliness. Henry Ford said genius is 2 percent inspiration and 98 percent perspiration. Tim Puchta's corollary is that after getting good fruit, winemaking comes down to 2 percent inspiration and 98 percent sanitation.

The Stark Star underwent a slow, traditional fermentation at about 64 degrees. Tim used *prise de mousse* yeast and left skin contact for three or four weeks. Tim noted that the juice has a very pleasant aroma, a trait noted by winemakers nearly 100 years ago.

"I was surprised the wine came up with a light color, as nice and dark as the skins were," Tim said. "We extracted every bit of pigment from the skins, yet I feel there's still not enough pigment and plan to blend a little more to achieve the color I want."

A pretty blush color is something winemakers work to achieve when making a blush wine. Since the Stark Star by itself produces the perfect blush color, Tim is thinking how he will vinify the grape next year. He may also ferment at a little warmer temperature to see if he can't "blow off some heaviness."

This year, Tim is making a light, Chianti-like red wine. To tone down the heavy Labrusca character, he blended in two French hybrids—Bellandais, a Seibel French hybrid, and Seyval Blanc—and he plans to sweeten it a little.

"There's a lot of nose, but not a lot of taste when it's totally dry," he observed.

Adam Puchta Winery's Stark Star is made to drink young.

And yes, Mr. Stark, we want to learn more about your "beautiful and attractive grape." With the Stark Star already pushing buds for its 100th-year crop, I believe some tasting and discussion is required.

Gentlemen, you have our attention.

From Wine Country Journal, *spring 1991*

EXPLORING STEELVILLE
Peaceful Bend Vineyards & Winery

B & Bs • Eats • Lodging • Parking • Post Office • Restrooms • Shopping
Chamber of Commerce: (573) 775-5533

Originally settled in the 1830s, Steelville was originally named Davey. Later, the town was renamed in honor of James Steel, an early settler. The name was on the mark because the town eventually became an important center for the mining of high-grade iron ore.

The town is surrounded by national and state forest land that is intersected by several streams and rivers. There are several opportunities for hiking and mountain biking in the surrounding forests and the areas rivers are open for floating and fishing.

The 1990 census named Steelville the National Population Center. This designation means that if the entire population of the United States was placed on a flat map of the country (assuming they all weighed the same and no one moved), the map would balance at a point 9.7 miles south of Steelville.

Local attractions include a country music show, a bluegrass festival, camping, dude ranches, golf courses, riding stables, RV parks, riverside resorts, caves, a trout park and several antique shops.

Bed & Breakfasts

Frisco Street Bed
1 (888) 229-4247

Wicker House
(573) 775-2166

Misty Forest
(573) 775-3126

Lodging
Wildwood Springs
1 (800) 554-3746

Annual Events

April: Dogwood Festival
May: Summerfest and Car Show
June: Spring Junk-A-Rama, Benefit Golf Tournament
July: Freedom Festival
September: Harvest Festival, Parade and Fall Rodeo
October: Fall Junk-A-Rama and Quilt & Doll Show
November: Christmas in the Country
December: Children's Christmas Pageant

PEACEFUL BEND
VINEYARDS & WINERY

Route 2, Box 544, Steelville, MO 65565
(573) 775-3000
Hours of Operation:
Monday through Saturday 10 a.m. to 5:30 p.m.
Sunday noon to 6 p.m.
Closed major holidays.

HOW TO GET THERE: From I-44 take Exit 208 at Cuba. Go south on Highway 19 for 8 miles to Highway 8. Go west 2 miles on Highway 8 to Route T. Peaceful Bend is 2 miles on the left. Watch for the signs. (The Cuba Highway 19 turnoff is just a one-hour drive west of I-270.)

Since 1964, Peaceful Bend Vineyards & Winery has been a leader in the Missouri wine industry. It was in that year that the vineyard operators at Peaceful Bend undertook the experimental planting of several acres of vineyard with French-American hybrid grapes. This experiment determined which grape varieties could produce quality yields in the unpredictable and sometimes harsh weather conditions of Missouri. From the end of Prohibition to the 1970s, nearly

all Missouri wines were made from native Missouri grapes. With this in mind it is easy to see how these experiments were bound to revolutionize the wine industry of Missouri.

Since 1972, the folks at Peaceful Bend have been making quality wines with what they believe to be the best scientific process coupled with old world care and patience. Owner Judy DuBose, along with her daughter and chief vintner, Aleta, make their wines only from grapes grown in their own vineyards and only in limited quantities. With their 7-acre vineyard, they produce about 4,000 gallons of wine annually.

PEACEFUL BEND WINE LIST

Current Offerings:

BLACKBERRY DRY: A semi-dry, dark wine made from 100 percent field-grown blackberries. 2 percent residual sugar.

BLACKBERRY SWEET: A very sweet, rich dessert wine made from 100 percent field-grown blackberries. 12 percent residual sugar.

CONCORD: A moderately sweet red wine produced from 100 percent Missouri-grown Concord grapes. Has a fresh fruity flavor. 7 percent residual sugar.

COUTOIS: A dry white wine made from primarily Seyval Blanc and Vignoles grapes. No residual sugar. Silver medal winner.

FORCHE-A-RENAULT: A dry mellow red table wine. The blend of French and American hybrids gives it an extra softness. Oak-aged. 1 percent residual sugar.

HONEY MIST: Dry Vidal with a touch of Missouri honey. 2 percent residual sugar.

HUZZAH VALLEY: (pronounced WHO-zaw) A semi-sweet dark rosé made from French hybrid and native American grapes. 4 percent residual sugar.

MERAMEC: A very dry robust red wine made from Cynthiana and Chambourcin grapes. Aged a minimum of 1 year in oak. No residual sugar.

RAVISSANT BLANC: A semi-dry premium white wine. Verdelet and Vidal French hybrid grapes are used to produce this white wine with a crisp fruity taste. 1.25 percent residual sugar. Gold medal winner.

RIVER RAT RED: Our extra sweet red wine developed for river floaters. Packaged in a plastic bottle perfect for paddlers. 10 percent residual sugar.

SCARLET BLUSH: A slightly tart rosé wine, blended of separately fermented red and white French and American hybrid grapes. 3 percent residual sugar.

SWEET RIVER RED: A moderately sweet red wine made from French and American grapes. 8 percent residual sugar.

SWEET RIVER WHITE: A moderately sweet white wine made from French and American grapes. 7 percent residual sugar. Gold medal winner.

VIEUX ROUGE: A semi-dry, red wine made from 4 varieties of French hybrid grapes, Baco Noir and Leon Millot. Stainless aged. 1.75 percent residual sugar.

WHITTENBERG CREEK: A fruity semi-sweet wine from five varieties of French and American hybrid grapes. 4 percent residual sugar. Bronze medal winner.

YADKIN CREEK: A semi-sweet red wine made from Chelois and Landot grapes. Oak aged to achieve its unique taste. 4 percent residual sugar.

SWEET RIVER WHITE

Sweet White Table Wine

PRODUCED AND BOTTLED BY

Peaceful Bend Vineyard

STEELVILLE MISSOURI

Special Section:
THE UBIQUITOUS WINE BARREL

Missouri's abundance of white oak in the Ozark Highlands region makes our state an important manufacturer of oak barrels. Although only three cooperages within the state continue this ancient barrel-making trade, their efforts define many subtleties of Missouri's finest wines.

The most obvious reason barrels have been the traditional choice for storing wine is that they can be rolled from place to place. A barrel's special shape also allows it to absorb most impacts without smashing. But the major reason barrels play such an important part in winemaking history is not so readily visible.

Premium white and red wines are frequently matured in oak barrels to impart subtle flavors to the wine and add a healthy finish. Just as dominant grape varieties provide standards for wine production, white oak has endured as the wood of choice for barrels. In addition to the resilient nature of white oak, the wood contains natural sealants, called tyloses, that help to prevent leakage. For wine, tight barrels are essential—they simply must not leak!

Though the shape of the barrel, or cask, has remained relatively unchanged for close to 3,000 years, the wine casks used today are constructed to much more precise specifications. In fact, casks used by Missouri wineries are required to be accurate within a few tenths of a gallon. This precision is required in order for vintners to be able to produce premium wines that meet their exacting standards.

Just as the vintner is following meticulous steps towards creating award-winning wine, the cooper is also following exacting specifications honed by generations of craftsmen. The first, and perhaps the most important, step is the selection of the oak. Oaks that yield premium barrels are sound, have straight grains and are fairly free of knots and branch stubs. Second, the wood is milled, yielding bolts, or roughed-out barrel pieces. These are then refined to become the staves of the barrel. Staves are the thin pieces of wood, typically 4 inches or less in width, that form the body of the barrel.

As the barrel is raised, or begins to take shape, the staves are cupped to make them adhere. The staves are then assembled into metal truss hoops. Once in place, the barrels are heated over a small fire to set the shape of the cask.

Next, the barrels are charred on the inside. A torch shoots flames through the barrel until the right degree of charring is attained. This critical step is variable. Often the buyer of the barrel predetermines the degree of charring, which will greatly affect the finish of the wines stored within it.

Then a small groove, called a croze, is machined into the barrel so that it will accept the end pieces, called headings. Headings are then put on. These are most often flat-cut from oak timber then attached using flagging, a form of grass that helps to seal the seams. With the ends in place, the truss hoops are removed and permanent hoops are added. Next, the bung hole, or filling hole, is drilled through a selected stave and *voilà*, a barrel is born.

EXPLORING LICKING

Reis Winery

Eats • Lodging • Post Office • Montauk State Park
Licking Chamber of Commerce: (573) 674-2510

Originally called Buffalo Lick or The Lick, this rural Missouri town was named for a nearby buffalo salt lick. Settlers started moving into the area in 1826, and by 1857 the area was surveyed as a townsite. Twenty-one years later the town was officially incorporated.

This area took quite a licking during the Civil War, as both Confederate and Union troops raided farms and homes. After the war, few structures were still intact. Residents had to start one of several rebuilding efforts in the town's history. The second blow came in 1880 when a tornado hit the town. Numerous fires also destroyed various sections of town during its early years.

One aspect of the town that has endured is the town newspaper, the *Licking News,* which is nearly 125 years old.

While out exploring Missouri wine country, make sure you make it to Montauk State Park, located approximately 12 miles east of town. This park offers plenty of outdoor recreation. Here, the Ozark Highland's rich flora and fauna combine with spring-fed waterways to produce some gorgeous scenery.

Montauk State Park is home to several springs that feed an estimated 43 million gallons of water a day into the Current River—the headwaters of this fabulous river are located in the northern section of the park. Cool, clear, spring-fed waters course through the park and offer great fishing opportunities.

Throughout the year, trout fishing draws anglers from across the Midwest. The official trout season runs from March 1 to October 31, but a catch-and-release season continues throughout the winter. If you don't have time to try your luck with a fishing rod, the Conservation Department also manages a trout hatchery here that is fun to tour. Bring some change so you can feed the fish.

In addition to trout fishing, hiking, nature study and camping opportunities abound. Montauk State Park also has cabins, a motel, campsites (many with electrical hook-ups) and a modern dining lodge. Be sure to visit the turn of the century grist mill, too.

For information about the park or to reserve a cabin, room or campsite, call the Montauk Park Office at (314) 548-2201.

Motel
Tarry Inn
(573) 674-2114

REIS WINERY

20199 Highway CC, Licking, MO 65542
(573) 674-3763
Hours of Operation:
Open daily (call before you come)

HOW TO GET THERE: Reis Winery is located 28 miles south of Rolla. Take Highway 63 to Junction C, then go left (east) 4 miles to the winery and vineyards (at Maples). Then look for their vineyard and sign.

Perched atop the Ozark Plateau are the vineyards of Reis Winery. At an elevation of 1,350 feet, the 8-acre vineyard owned by Val and Joy Reis produces more than 30 varieties of native and French hybrid grapes.

The grapes are picked by hand at the peak of ripeness and handled with care to ensure they produce the highest quality wine. With painstaking attention to detail, vintners Val and Joy Reis oversee every step in the transformation. Their red wines are produced the old-fashioned way, with the skins and in oak barrels, while the white wines are aged in stainless steel tanks. Bring along a picnic and enjoy an afternoon in the sun at Reis.

Nearby: The spring and fall are also good seasons to visit the nearby Montauk State Park (see p. 129) which offers trout fishing, camping and lodging.

REIS WINE LIST

Current Offerings:
BLACKBERRY: A sweet wine made from locally produced blackberries.
BURGUNDY: A hearty, rich-tasting dry red wine.
CONCORD: A sweet red wine with a fruity Concord grape flavor.
HARVEST GOLD: German-style white dessert wine
HARVEST RED: Similar to a sweet port wine.
LEON MILLOT: A robust, full-bodied, aromatic dry red wine.
MOUNTAIN RED WINE: A light-bodied, semi-sweet red.
MOUNTAIN WHITE WINE: A semi-sweet wine.
RHINE: A delicate, semi-dry white wine.
SEYVAL BLANC: A complex dry white wine with a distinctive bouquet.
STRAWBERRY: A sweet wine made from locally produced strawberries.
VIDAL: A pleasant, semi-dry white wine.

R E I S

MISSOURI

RHINE

White Dinner Wine Produced From Select French Hybrid Grapes Grown at Our Vineyards in the Missouri Ozark Plateau at an Elevation of 1,350 ft.

PRODUCED AND BOTTLED BY
REIS WINERY, BW-MO-108, LICKING, MISSOURI
ALCOHOL 11% BY VOLUME

Ozark Mountains Region

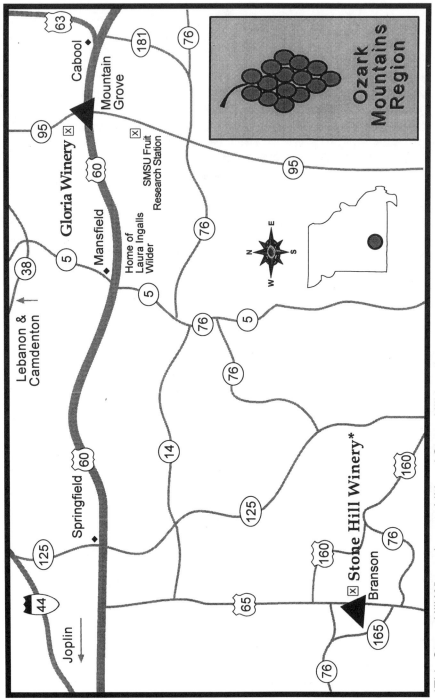

*This Stone Hill Winery is an additional Stone Hill location.

OZARK MOUNTAINS REGION

This region includes the two southern-most wineries, Gloria Winery & Vineyard and Stone Hill's Branson Winery. Southwest Missouri State University's Fruit Experiment Station in Mountain Grove is also in this region. This is where much of the grape and wine research for the state takes place.

EXPLORING MOUNTAIN GROVE
Gloria Winery & Vineyard

Antiques • B & Bs • Eats • Gas • Lodging • Parking • Restrooms
Area Chamber of Commerce: (417) 926-4135

In 1882 the Kansas City, Springfield & Memphis Railroad was slated to miss the town of Hickory Springs. So the town leaders made the economically sensible decision and moved everything to a new site adjacent to the tracks. Several other smaller communities in the vicinity were eventually consolidated and re-named Mountain Grove.

Today, Mountain Grove is primarily an agricultural community with a population of close to 4,000. The town is surrounded by wooded hills and open meadows well suited for the outdoor enthusiast. Much of the land in this area is part of the Mark Twain National Forest and is open to campers, hikers and mountain bikers. There are also several miles of streams that are perfect for canoeing and many beautiful lakes for fishing.

While in the area you might like to take a spin past the State Fruit Experiment Station Research Campus. Faurot Hall, a building located on the grounds of the State Fruit Experiment Station, is included on the National Historic Register along with Mountain Grove's Central Park with its historic bandstand.

Or, take the old mill tour where you can see some of the nation's finest surviving pioneer water mills. To early settlers, water was the primary source of power. Mills were used to grind grain, to saw lumber and to perform other labor-intensive tasks. The visitors center provides maps to lead your exploration.

Laura Ingalls Wilder's home, where the "Little House" books were written, is located just a few miles west of Mountain Grove in Mansfield. In 1932, Laura published the first of her books, which describe the pioneering Ingalls and Wilder families during the 1870s – 1890s. All of the nine manuscripts were penned here at Rocky Ridge Farm. Walk through Laura's home—preserved as she left it in 1957—and tour the museum that includes Pa's fiddle and birthday cards from school children from around the world. The house is located one mile east of the Mansfield town square at 3068 Highway A in Mansfield. Tours are offered daily. Signs around town point you there, or call (417) 924-3626 for more information.

Lodging

Cedar Hill Farm	Days Inn
(417) 926-6535	(417) 926-3152
Best Western	Mountain Grove Motel
(417) 926-5555	(417) 926-6101

Restaurants

The Hayloft	The Triangle
(417) 926-6200	(417) 926-3715

Earl Hess has joined the harvest crew at Gloria four years running.

GLORIA WINERY & VINEYARD

11185 Stave Mill Road, Mountain Grove, MO 65711

(417) 926-6263

Hours of Operation:

Daily 11 a.m. to sundown

HOW TO GET THERE: Located on Highway 60 between Mountain Grove and Cabool, Gloria Winery & Vineyard is located near the intersection of Route MM and Highway 60—Watch for the signs!

The vigilant, almost paternal care of the 7.5-acre vineyard began in 1972 when Bill Toben planted the first vines. With the first commercial crush in 1991, he and his wife, Jane, opened the doors of their winery in 1992, producing 500 gallons of dry red wine. To this day, the operation has remained a small, family-run business.

"We live the business," says Jane. The Tobens have no employees—except during harvest—and plan to keep their winery small and personal. They average about five cars a day and don't encourage bus tours. "It's a wonderful, healthy lifestyle," she says.

Gloria wines are only available from their winery. They bottle about 1,000 gallons each year of eight varieties. They also sell some of their French hybrid grapes to area wineries like Cavern Springs and Bias Winery. Gloria specializes in hearty red, European-style table wines. Unlike some other vineyards, Gloria Winery doesn't use oak barrels. Stainless steel tanks are used for maturation.

"We like to produce fresh fruity reds, which may not garner international acclaim—but they are good to drink," Jane said.

Jane attributes their fine wines to their small size, which she says lets them harvest grapes at their peak. "There's no lag time on the grape at all," Jane said. "We pick them that morning and have them fermenting by 1 p.m."

Like many other small wineries, nothing goes to waste. For the last five years, they have been selling clippings to a nursery in New York State. The clippings are then sold to vineyards throughout the world. Other clippings and grape stems get used for mulch.

Inside, the winery offers other products to complement their wines from local cheese and sausage producers.

Jane says home winemaking is becoming more popular and an increasing number of what she calls "wine groupies" come to her vineyard each year to pick and press their own grapes.

GLORIA WINE LIST

Current Offerings:
CHAMBOURCIN: Off-dry, full-bodied red varietal from the Chambourcin grape.
FLORA: Semi-sweet blush, pink and fruity.
IMPO ROSÉ: Slightly sweet red rosé.
OLD MILL RED: Sweet, fruity, dessert-style sipping wine named for the historical lumber and grist mills in the area.
OZARKA: Full-bodied, semi-sweet red.
ROUGE AUX ARCS: Hearty, burgundy-style blended dry red. Lively and complex.
ST. VINCENT: Dry, red varietal. Light-bodied and lively with hints of chocolate and berry flavors.
VILLARD NOIR: Dry, red varietal wine. Soft and fruity.

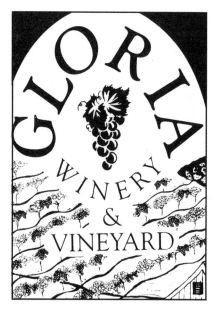

Special Essay:
WHO'S GLORIA?

by Jane Toben

Once upon a time a farm boy in northern Missouri watched his grandfather tend a small vineyard and turn the harvest into wine for family meals. The boy was fascinated by the process and came to know in his heart that one day he, too, would grow grapes and make wine.

As the boy grew into manhood he continued to learn winemaking from his grandfather. And as he learned, he began to dream of his own vineyard and winery. He began making plans and set a goal in his mind.

But, as happens to so many dreams, the vicissitudes of life demanded a different path. Higher education, service to his country, then the responsibilities of a young family kept him very busy. Even so, the calling beckoned him. He planted a few vines in his backyard and made a little wine.

Years passed. Now a grandfather, the man realized time was growing short and he must fulfill his dream. He set out to find a proper location for his project and searched the country far and wide. Then he chose a special spot in the Ozark hills—just right for a vineyard and winery. Though the task before him loomed monumental, for he was working alone, he set his heart to the call and his hands to the planting of grapes—and was happy.

At the same time, in the same county, just a few rolling hills away, lived a strong, resourceful woman, who tended a garden, baked her own bread and celebrated the quiet country evenings with a glass of her own homemade wine. She was happy but concerned for her future, when her children would be grown and gone—and she, too, would be facing life alone.

By and by, seemingly through divine guidance, these two people struck up an acquaintance. As time passed this grew into a friendship and then, suddenly—blossomed into the miracle of love. When the man told the woman of his dream, she embraced them both and took them to her heart. From that day forward they worked as one towards the fulfillment of the dream they now shared.

And so, like a precious, late-born child, GLORIA WINERY & VINEYARD is the dream become reality. The name is taken from the phrase "Gloria in Excelsis Deo," to remind all who share in the dream that they are stewards of the gifts of grapes and wine, and thankful for the time, talent and love that the Maker has bestowed upon them.

EXPLORING BRANSON

Stone Hill Winery–Branson

B & Bs • Bikes • Crafts • Eats • Lodging • Parking • Post Office • Restrooms
Branson Area Chamber of Commerce: (417) 334-4136

Branson was nothing more than a quiet Ozark hamlet until the early 1900s. With the publication of the novel *Shepherd of the Hills*, however, things began to change. This book, written by Harold Bell Wright, flooded the community with curiosity seekers interested in the Ozarks. Visitors' camps housed many of these early tourists.

The completion of the Ozark Beach Dam near Forsythe in 1913 greatly increased recreation on the newly formed Lake Taneycomo. Then, in the 1950s, Table Rock Lake was formed by another dam. Fishermen and boaters increased their visits and haven't ceased since.

The 1960s brought another new attraction to Branson—one that was to change the town beyond its wildest dreams. When Hugo and Mary Herchend opened their small attraction atop Marvel Cave and called it Silver Dollar City, little did they realize what they were giving birth to. Next came the production of "Shepherd of the Hills," which was located on the site where the characters in Wright's novel originated.

With these two pillars of attraction firmly established, other acts followed. The first music act to hit the town was a troupe calling itself The Baldknobbers. Their success in staging an Ozark country repertoire led to the infusion of additional acts.

Several regionally famous acts increased the number of visitors to Branson, but it wasn't until the Roy Clark Celebrity Theatre opened in 1983 that the town really began to attract national attention.

Today, there are scores of things to do in Branson. From music and drama to rides and recreation, you'll find more to do here than you could possibly accomplish in a single day's visit.

Branson Visitors Center is the best place to get started before exploring Branson. From Highway 65, take the Highway 248 Exit and follow the signs. The visitors center and chamber of commerce are right next to one another. Their friendly staff will provide you with all of the maps and information you may need. As for places to stay, there are more hotels in Branson than you can shake a stick at. Contact the Tourism Information number listed above for a complete listing.

Reprinted from Lee N. Godley and Patricia O'Rourke.
Daytrip Missouri. *Aphelion Publications, Fulton, Mo, 1996*

STONE HILL WINERY—BRANSON

601 State Highway 165, Branson, MO 65616
(417) 334-1897
Hours of Operation:
Monday through Saturday 8:30 a.m. to dusk
Sunday 11 a.m. to 6 p.m. Tours start every 15 minutes.

HOW TO GET THERE: Stone Hill Winery in Branson is located on Highway 165, 2 blocks south of Highway 76 west.

Stone Hill's Branson winery offers one of the best free tours of any winery. You are led through the history of winemaking with interesting videos and memorabilia, and bottlers give demonstrations that, in addition to being informative, are also very entertaining.

After the tour, the tasting room has samples of Stone Hill's award-winning wines. Each sample is presented with interesting background information and serving hints. There's plenty of grape juice for the kids (and adults). Of course there's also a gift shop to browse, for that one-of-a-kind wine-related gift.

Five-foot-high oak barrels that were housed in a St. Louis monastery, and thus survived Prohibition, now rest in Branson's Stone Hill location. Other than the winemaking and wine-tasting demonstrations, there are no vineyards or large-scale wine production facilities here. As one tour guide says, "All we can grow on the hills here are rocks." If this visit piques your interest in Missouri wine country, a visit to Stone Hill in Hermann is definitely in order.

STONE HILL WINE LIST
(Please see Stone Hill's Hermann listing.)

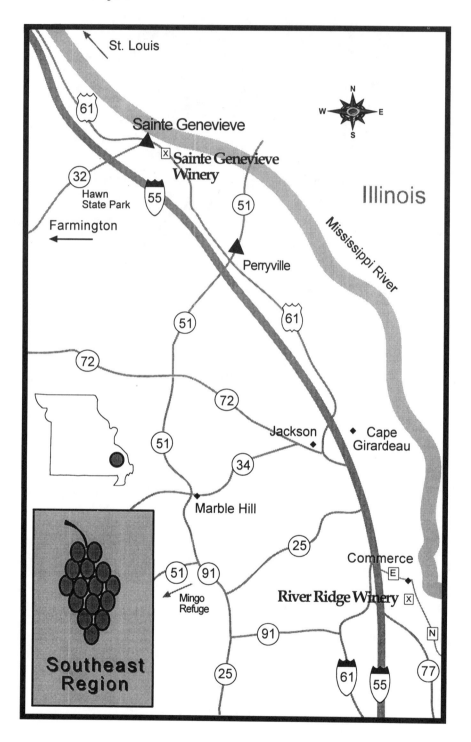

SOUTHEAST
REGION

The southeastern wine region includes a visit to Missouri's oldest permanent settlement and some great drives through gorgeous rolling Ozark terrain.

This corner of the state was a particular highlight for me, given its rich, early French history. In fact, Ste. Genevieve holds a full quarter of all surviving French Colonial architecture in the Western Hemisphere.

EXPLORING STE. GENEVIEVE

Sainte Genevieve Winery

Eats • Historic Homes • Lodging • Museums
Parking • Post Office • Restrooms
Ste. Genevieve Tourist Information Center: (573) 883-7097 or 1 (800) 373-7007

Sainte Genevieve, regarded as the oldest permanent settlement in the state, was established in the 1730s and named in honor of a female saint—the patron saint of Paris. Founded on the western bank of the Mississippi River, the town marked the French foothold on the western frontier. The population of the town grew quickly because of its convenient location to the river, access to Ozark lead mines, abundant salt springs and rich gumbo soil.

In 1762, the territory was transferred to Spain and the young town became an outpost for the Spanish government. The French American town continued to grow rapidly and tolerated a wide mix of cultural influences. Life was more communal than that of their English counterparts, and French and Native Americans lived in relative harmony.

Though it was the fertile river bottoms that allowed pioneers to thrive, the Mississippi River also devastated the community several times. One of the most severe floods came in 1785, when the city was covered by more than fifteen feet of water. The town was then moved to its current location, a bit farther from the river. It now sits beyond the reaches of all but the highest of floods. In later years, as river traffic and mining interest decreased, agriculture and German settlement helped the town survive into the 20th century.

The mix of commerce and cultures, both then and now, make Ste. Genevieve truly unique. Today many bed & breakfasts, restaurants, antique and specialty shops add to the experience of visiting the largest collection of 18th century Creole, or French American, structures in the Western Hemisphere. A good place to begin exploring is the Great River Road Interpretive Center located at 66 South Main Street. They provide a complete listing of historic homes and museums. Their phone number is 1 (800) 373-7007.

Be sure and visit the Bolduc House, constructed around 1770. The nearby Felix Valle House State Historic Site is also a must see. This vertical log house dates to 1790. Many other 19th century churches and homes also add to the charm and appeal of the town's central square and its rich history.

The Steiger Haus Bed & Breakfast here is also worth noting. Instead of a typical night's stay, guests are treated to an evening of murder mystery theater as guests try to figure out "who dunnit." Invite a house-full of your friends and spend a night unlike any other. Call (573) 883-5881 for more information.

Nearby: Visit Hawn State Park on Route 32, (573) 883-3603. There are also trails in the Whispering Pines and Pickle Creek natural areas close nearby.

Bed & Breakfasts

Chateau Sainte Genevieve
(573) 883-2800

Inn St. Gemme Beauvais
(573) 883-5744 or 1 (800) 818-5744

Rocky Ridge Ranch B & B
(573) 483-2057

Jon Hael Gasthaus
(573) 883-5881

The Creole House B & B
(573) 883-7171 or 1 (800) 275-6041

Southern Hotel
(573) 883-3493

Falk House
(573) 883-5881

Steiger Haus
1 (800) 814-5881

Annual Events

February: King's Ball—a 200-year-old tradition
April: Annual Spring House Tour
June: Sainte Genevieve Quilt Show
July: Bastille Days
August: Jour de Fete—the area's largest craft fair
October: Fall Harvest Festival
December: Annual Country Christmas Walk, Historic French Christmas

The Bolduc House, built in 1770, is regarded as the most authentically restored French-American house in the nation. It is open for tours April through November.

SAINTE GENEVIEVE WINERY

245 Merchant Street, Ste. Genevieve, MO 63670
(573)883-2800
Hours of Operation:
Open daily 11 a.m. to 5 p.m.

HOW TO GET THERE: The winery is located in Ste. Genevieve's French Colonial Historical District on Merchant Street, between Second and Third Street.

Established in 1984, the Sainte Genevieve Winery is located in a 5,000-square-foot, turn-of-the-century home. The winery features a complete line of premium and traditional wines from fresh grapes and fruit that is either grown in their 13-acre vineyard or purchased from area vineyards and orchards.

The winery and vineyard was started by Chris and Hope Hoffmeister on their 400-acre farm. One short year later, the winery outgrew the small farm building in which it was originally housed and the Hoffmeisters relocated to the current location. The winery's growth has not slowed since its inception and its owners are always planning for expansion. This sort of popularity is an accurate gauge of the quality you will find at this picturesque winery.

The second floor of this beautiful home has been transformed into a bed & breakfast called Chateau Ste. Genevieve. The elegant rooms are decorated in Queen Ann décor. Guests will spend the evening with the Hoffmeisters, tasting Missouri wines and nibbling on appetizers. A delicious gourmet breakfast is served in the morning.

When you visit the Sainte Genevieve Winery you will have a chance to share in the Hoffmeister's love of wine. Stop in for a free tasting.

SAINTE GENEVIEVE WINE LIST

Current Offerings:
AMOREAUX: White dessert wine.
BEAUVAIS: Dry Beaujolais-style.
BLACKBERRY WINE
BLUEBERRY WINE
BOLDUC: Semi-dry, Beaujolais-style red. Ruby color with a fruity finish.
CHATEAU STE. GENEVIEVE: Semi-dry white with a slightly sweet finish.
CHERRY WINE
CHRISTMAS PLUM (Only available during the holidays season)
CONCORD: Sweet, full-bodied red.
ELDERBERRY WINE
LA ROSE ROSÉ: Semi-sweet blush wine.
RED RASPBERRY WINE
STRAWBERRY WINE
STE. GEMME: Semi-dry white with an oak touch.
VALLE RHINE: Light, semi-sweet white Rhine-style wine.
VIDAL BLANC: Dry white with distinctive varietal aroma and flavor.

EXPLORING COMMERCE

River Ridge Winery

B & B • Parking • Post Office • Restrooms
Commerce Museum: (573) 264-3960

Commerce is possibly the oldest community west of the Mississippi still in its original location. While you won't find much about this place in the history books, there are a lot of stories here waiting to be told. The Commerce Historical Society publishes regular newsletters—about 24 pages in length—and is even conducting an archaeological dig of a pre–Civil War site. The society's newsletters and recovered artifacts can be found at the Commerce Museum.

On the next page is a brief history written by Dixie High. Mrs. High and her husband Jack are transplants to Commerce from Las Vegas, Nevada. She serves as: caretaker to the museum, editor of the *Commerce Newsletter*, secretary of the Commerce Historical Society, member of the Scott County Tourism Committee and secretary of the Commerce Better Community Club. In her spare time she's a freelance photographer.

Bed & Breakfast
Anderson House
(573) 264-4123 or 1 (800) 705-1317

Special Essay:
COMMERCE
by Dixie High

The sign states it was founded in 1790—though there's a question about when it was first settled, since a map printed in London shows one of the Pittman's settlements was here prior to 1770 . . . Commerce sits on its original site. Even with all the floods, no levee or floodwall has ever been built to protect the town, or to obscure the beautiful view of the showboats and the barges going up and down the Mississippi. Once the site of major industry and one of the main ports for boats, barges and showboats, now Commerce is struggling to stay afloat and can only wave to the river traffic since the docks are gone.

Visitors to Commerce have included the Czar of Russia, and Bill Cody's family and sister-in-law were from here. A lot of citizens prior to 1900 came to Commerce and left for other parts once they got their start here. Once the site of many hotels, restaurants, bowling alleys, movie houses, doctors, lawyers, judges—and Scott County's first newspaper—now it has one bed & breakfast, one tavern, an auto repair shop, two churches, a community hall and a museum in a 100-year-old church.

Commerce is on the south end of the bluffs known as Crowley's Ridge. The King's Highway originally went along the river through Commerce, but the floods made upkeep too expensive so it was changed to Benton. But one can still see some of the old roadbed if you walk along the river just north of Commerce. The railroad came here and many residents can remember the old depot, though all that remains are a few iron spikes in the dirt.

Commerce was the site of a "retaliation" during the Civil War. On August 10, 1861, Captain Price of the Missouri State Guard received a letter from Colonel Marsh. It said that if the people in Commerce or their property, were attacked that night, the hostages would be killed and bitter revenge would be taken upon certain persons . . . In 1863 an average of only $1.59 worth of food and supplies could be made per person per month, due to the war.

Some of the homes destroyed in the FEMA flood buyout in 1996 were built with cypress wood more than 100 years ago. But it was wrecking machines, not the mighty Mississippi that finally pushed them over. Only 13 people left because of the FEMA buyout and more lots are being cleared for some new homes.

While some old homes were destroyed, many others continue to stand as monuments to the people that worked so hard over 100 years ago to help build this river town.

RIVER RIDGE WINERY
P.O. Box 118, Commerce, MO 63742
(573) 264-3712 or (573) 264-2747
Hours of Operation:
Open daily noon to 6 p.m.
Closed Christmas and Easter

HOW TO GET THERE: Take I-55 south from Cape Girardeau to Route E. Travel east on Route E and then north on County Road 321 at Commerce. The winery will be on your right.

Located on the scenic Crowley's Ridge at the Mississippi River, River Ridge Winery is located in a farmhouse which dates back to 1894. The winery was established in 1993.

Winemaker Jerry Smith and his wife Joannie, operate one of Missouri's smallest wineries and vineyards. Smith says the people in and around Commerce have welcomed and supported his vineyard. They produce up to 4,000 gallons annually, and tend a 4-acre vineyard on the hill behind the winery. In the next few years they plan to increase production and add several red wines to their list.

He is particulary proud of his dry white wine Serendipity.

"If you like Chardonnay, you'll like Serendipity better," he says.

They grow several varieties of French hybrid grapes, including Vignoles, Vidal and Seyval. They also have contracts to buy other varieties such as Chambourcin, Chardonnay and Merlot.

Hand-tended grapes are used to make River Ridge's high-quality dry and semi-dry table wines. As many as five years may be needed from harvest until they are served. Smith ages his wines in Missouri white oak barrels.

Smith says he wanted to start a vineyard and make wine for most of his adult life. A retired Navy fighter pilot, Smith and his wife have lived in New Orleans, California and Greece. Though River Ridge is currently the only winery this far south, Smith is happy to be finally realizing his dream, and also taking part in the rejuvenation of Missouri wines.

Drop by the winery for a complimentary tasting or call ahead and reserve a time for a full service dinner. The winery also has a selection of cheese, sausage and bread for an afternoon picnic by the river or in the vineyard. While visiting River Ridge, be sure to browse their showroom full of unique wine-related items. They are open for weddings, private wine tastings and special dinners.

RIVER RIDGE WINE LIST

Current Offerings:
CHAMBOURCIN: Dry red aged in oak.
CYNTHIANA: Dry red aged in oak.
SERENDIPITY: Dry white aged in oak.
VIDAL: Dry white aged in oak.
VIGNOLES: Dry white aged in oak.
VILLARD BLANC: Semi-dry white.
VINS GRIS: Semi-dry blush.

THE BEST & THE BIGGEST

The Best

Best-in-Class Winners at the
1996 Missouri State Fair Wine Competition

Governor's Cup Winner:
Augusta Winery—1993 Cynthiana

Best Dry White	Stone Hill Winery—Barrel Fermented Seyval
Best Off-Dry White	Hermannhof Winery—1995 Vignoles
	Augusta Winery—1995 Seyval
	Blumenhof Vineyards & Winery—1995 Vignoles
Best Dry Red	Augusta Winery—1993 Cynthiana
Best Off-Dry Red	Montelle Winery—Chambourcin
Best Sparkling	Stone Hill Winery—Golden Spumante

The Biggest

By gallons of Missouri wine sold, retail and wholesale

Stone Hill Winery—125,349
St. James Winery—52,905
Mount Pleasant Wine Company—35,750
Les Bourgeois Winery & Vineyards—29,510
Hermannhof Winery—16,127
Montelle Winery—11,735
Winery of the Little Hills—9,799
Blumenhof Vineyards & Winery—8,130
Augusta Winery—7,932
Sainte Genevieve Winery—7,368

From Missouri Grape and Wine Program,
Missouri Department of Agriculture, January 1996

Dr. Phillip Weinberger hopes to open Montserrat Vineyards as soon as he can navigate the necessary paperwork.

BUDDING WINERIES
RIPE FOR EXPLORATION

Here's a list of wineries planning to open their doors soon. Since plans often change in the world of viticulture, call before visiting. For a complete listing of new wineries, call the Grape and Wine Program in Jefferson City at 1 (800) 392-WINE.

Coming soon:
Stonehaus Farms Vineyard & Winery
Ken and Carol Euritt
24607 Northeast Colbern Road
Lee's Summit, MO 64086
(816) 524-7703

Old Jamestown Winery
John Weese
1 Old Jamestown Road
St. Louis County, MO 63034
(314) 741-3784

Ponticello Winery
Bito Ponticello
Route 1, Box 129A
Hermann, MO 65041
(573) 437-3994

WINE OUTLETS

I f you are looking for a "one stop" shop to purchase a variety of Missouri wines, a wine outlet may be the way to go. Most offer an assortment of Missouri wines and special edible fare. These places can be a great way to relax along a trip through the state or can be a destination in and of themselves. Don't overlook these unique establishments—they are sure to offer something that will make your wine tour memorable.

MT. PLEASANT WINERY—ABBEY VINEYARD
Cuba, MO 65453
(573) 885-2168 or (573) 885-2123
Hours of Operation:
Monday through Saturday 9 a.m. to 6 p.m.
Sunday 11 a.m. to 6 p.m.

HOW TO GET THERE: Located an hour southwest of St. Louis on I-44, two miles outside of Cuba.

The Mt. Pleasant Winery–Abbey Vineyard is situated on 14 acres with several spacious granite and redwood buildings. The Mt. Pleasant award-winning wines are produced from nearby vineyards. Cheese, sausage, honey, cider, grape juice, preserves and fresh fruit are sold when in season, along with a selection of other Missouri wines. The products of many Missouri artisans are also sold there.

STONE HILL WINERY—NEW FLORENCE
Route 1, Box 614, New Florence, MO 63363
(573) 835-2420
Hours of Operation:
Monday through Saturday 8:30 a.m. to dusk
Sunday 11 a.m. to dusk

HOW TO GET THERE: The Stone Hill-New Florence facility is located at the junction of I-70 and Highway 19.

This building houses the bottle-fermented champagne operation. Visitors can sample and purchase wines from the Stone Hill wine list along with items from the extensive gift shop.

STONE HILL WINE LIST
(Please see Stone Hill's Hermann listing.)

ROSATI WINERY

22050 State Road KK, St. James, MO 65559

(573) 265-6892

Hours of Operation:

Open daily 9 a.m. to 9 p.m.

HOW TO GET THERE: Rosati Winery is located on historic Route 66. Take I-44 to Route F (Exit 203), go west on the south service road for 2 miles and you're there. Rosati Winery is 4 miles from St. James, 9 miles from Cuba and 15 miles from Rolla.

Owned and operated by Marvin and Donna Rippelmeyer, the Rosati Winery is a standing reminder of the early Italian heritage of Rosati. The building was originally constructed in 1922 by the Knobview Co-op to help grape growers ship their goods by train to the St. Louis markets and beyond. In 1933, wine production began at the site and today, the early vats and stately oak barrels remain as monuments to their efforts.

Now, the Rosati Winery produces 2,000 gallons of Concord grape juice annually. In addition to grape juice, their wineshop offers a wide selection of Missouri wines. The Rosati Winery also has a country store that sells a variety of handcrafted Ozark products. Picnic supplies are available for you to enjoy an afternoon in their quiet wine garden. Rosati also features a large meeting room for catering and special functions and an adjoining bed & breakfast. A vineyard and horse farm tour can also be arranged for a nominal fee (minimum of 6 persons).

NEW WORLD GRAPES
An Introduction to Early Grape Cultivation
Compiled from *Vintage Missouri*
by Robert Scheef

Before their discovery of North America, Europeans knew of only one species of wine grapes, the classic varieties of *Vitis vinifera* ("wine bearing"). Along with such exotic botanical specimens as corn, tomatoes and tobacco, the grapevines found in North America presented a challenge in taxonomy to 17th century botanists, since there were more grape varieties growing naturally between the Atlantic and the Pacific than in any other place in the world.

A Foxy Flavor

The first colonists to settle Jamestown tried to make wine from the strange new grapes, that easily slipped free of their tough skins. They made wine—at least a drink enough like wine—to accompany their first Thanksgiving dinner. When crushed, these native grapes gave off a pungent aroma described as "foxy." For

some writers of the time the term simply meant "wild." For others, the word conveyed the odor of the animal's wet fur. Over time, "foxy" came to mean any strongly foreign taste or smell of wine, including an overpowering flavor of the grape.

Early attempts to cultivate imported varieties failed to an even greater degree than the trials with native grapes. Occasionally, the European vines lived into their third year and began yielding fruit, but they rarely matured to full-bearing age. *Vinifera* vines in the colonies seemed as tenuous as orchids in Antarctica. Mysterious pests and unknown plant diseases also decimated the fragile vines. Even Europe's most seasoned vintners were unable to grow *Vitis vinifera* in North America at this time.

Let the Grafting Begin . . .

In the 19th century viticulturists realized the country's tremendous potential for producing wine. They needed a vine resistant to weather and disease like the native varieties, but which yielded grapes with the qualities of the European varieties. To tap this potential, decades of experiments ensued, grafting and cross-pollinating between native and European vines. Simply by planting *vinifera* vines beside native *labrusca*, the process of toning down the foxy quality of the native species had begun.

In the early days of plant hybridization it took years, even decades, to develop a new plant strain. Standard procedure was to surgically cross-pollinate two grape plants, then work with the seeds that resulted. Results could not be determined until viable plant hybrids survived. And then, only after several years of cultivation would the plants reveal whether their fruit made acceptable wine.

The onset of Prohibition curtailed further research and nearly erased the life's work of early scientists. A few varieties, such as Munson's Muench grape, Jacob Rommel's Elvira and Nicholas Grein's Missouri Riesling, escaped the purge and survived to produce wine in Missouri after Prohibition.

Among pioneering, early viticulturists was Texan T.V. Munson, who developed more than 300 hybrids, two of which he named for his Missouri colleagues Friedrich Muench and Hermann Jaeger. Hermann Jaeger was a grape-breeder from Neosho, Missouri, who in 1867 advised French viticulturists to graft their *phylloxera*-devastated vineyards onto wild Ozark vine roots. He shipped them 17 carloads of rootings and was later awarded the Cross of the French Legion of Honor.

George Husmann of Hermann also spent part of his life looking for the perfect grape for Missouri soils. In 1866, the year after the Civil War, Husmann penned his first book, *The Native Grape and the Manufacture of American Wines.* Husmann, like Jaeger, also shipped millions of *phylloxera*-resistant vines from Missouri to re-establish European vineyards. In St. Louis, he founded the *Grape Culturist*, one of the earliest American periodicals on viticulture, and wrote several more books. Husmann was also the first professor of horticulture at the University of Missouri. He headed west in 1881 to become a winemaker in California's Napa valley. Once there, he helped to stamp out the *phylloxera* plague. He then produced prize-winning wines for the Talcoa Vineyard of Napa and the Oak Glen Vineyard of Chiles valley until his death in 1902. Even today, some of his experimental vines, named Dry Hill Beauty, still bloom in a vineyard near Hermann.

Today, at the Fruit Experiment Station in Mountain Grove, enologists continue to seek out hybrids suited to Missouri growing conditions. Two premises guide their work: to find the grape that will become what Chardonnay was to Burgundy; and to support viticulture as a profitable form of agriculture.

NATIVE GRAPE VARIETIES

A merican species have played a major role in the world of wine, as disease-resistant rootstock and breeding stock. Only one species, *Vitis rotundifolia*, makes drinkable wine without *vinifera* influence. This is called scuppernong or muscadine, a wine associated with the southern Atlantic states. All other so-called "native grapes" evolved as varieties either through chance pollination with *vinifera* or through experimentation

The following list treats separately varieties found in the wild from varieties bred with a purpose in mind. Many experts consider members of the latter group such as Elvira, Missouri Riesling, Niagara and Delaware to be native varieties—offspring of American parents. The recorded history of these grapes, however, suggests that they are actually engineered "American hybrids" and, thus, suitable for inclusion in the following section.

Catawba (*V. labrusca*) In the 1820s, Revolutionary War hero Major John Adlum of Maryland cultivated Catawba cuttings from a neighbor's garden. He named these vines after the Catawba River in North Carolina. In 1823 Adlum sent one of his early Catawba vintages to his friend, former president Thomas Jefferson. Catawba is durable and productive, though it is prone to fungal diseases. It is a good grape for juices or for adding a fruity character to blended wines.

Isabella (*V. labrusca*) William R. Prince (1795–1869), a horticulturist from New York, believed this vine originated in South Carolina. Named for the wife of an amateur winegrower, the Isabella became almost as widely planted as Catawba prior to the Civil War. In Hermann, Jacob Fugger vinted this grape to contribute to the city's first vintage in 1848. Regarded as one of the more promising *phylloxera*-resistant rootstocks, cuttings of Isabella traveled worldwide.

Concord (*V. labrusca*) In 1849 Ephraim Wales Bull of Concord, Massachusetts, propagated a prolific and hardy vine from wild *labrusca* seeds he had gathered near his home. Three years later he exhibited the Concord to the Massachusetts Horticultural Society. More than the Alexander, Isabella and Catawba, the Concord heralded the dawn of commercial winemaking in America. Horticulturists spread Concord cuttings like children trade sports cards and marbles.

Hermann's George Husmann received "a few eyes" of Concord from an Illinois grower in 1855. In his 1885 book, *American Grape Growing and Wine Making*, Husmann wrote:

> . . . *Will with skillful handling and a little artificial heat, make*
> *a wine of fair quality, of very enlivening and invigorating*
> *character, which is emphatically the "poor man's" drink, as*
> *it can be produced cheap and is just the beverage he needs,*
> *instead of the poisonous compounds called whiskey and brandy.*

Norton (*V. aestavalis*) The Norton, once regarded as the best grape for red wine, was cultivated by Dr. Daniel Norton of Virginia, who believed the vine was a chance cross between the *vinifera* Miller's Burgundy and the Bland grape, a *labrusca* variety. Critics of this genealogy, however, point out that these parents don't flower at the same time, making cross-pollination unlikely. The controversy of the plant's origins, like that of California's Zinfandel, cloaks this grape in mystery.

Hermann's early vintners sought an evaluation of one of their first Norton vintages from Nicholas Longworth, recognized in his time as "the father of American grape culture." Repeating his earlier dim assessment of the Norton grape, Longworth judged the wine to be unpleasant. Husmann took the opposite stance on the Norton's future:

> *There is perhaps no other grape which has given such uniform satisfaction as this and although I have warmly praised and recommended it from the first, I have seen no reason to retract a single word which I have said in its favor . . .*

Cynthiana (*V. aestivalis*) Like the Norton, the source of the Cynthiana grape lurks in mystery. Many experts consider them to be one and the same grape. Many Missouri winemakers believed Cynthiana would become America's grape for red wine. In 1883, the Bushberg Catalogue proudly announced that the Isidor Bush & Son and Meissner Cynthiana had won the First Medal of Merit at the world exposition in Vienna. The next year French experts at the Congrès de Montpellier voiced unequivocal praise. They described the Cynthiana of Mr. Bush as "a red wine of fine color, rich in body and alcohol, reminding us of old Roussillon wine," an accolade they bestowed also on the wine of "Poschel & Sherer," the founders of Hermann's Stone Hill Wine Company.

GRAPE FACT

Laid to rest by science

There's a controversy in Missouri's tasting rooms that is as old as the vines. Some vintners believe that Norton and Cynthiana are two distinct varieties of grape vines, that one came from Virginia, the other from Arkansas . . . But, of course, there are other connoisseurs who will attest, with equal certainty, that these grapes are the same. The people who say we have two names for one grape are now supported with results of recent protein analysis, which show virtually identical compositions. So perhaps this perennial bone of relatively amicable contention, will finally be buried—along with so many other myths, wives' tales and other "flat earth" notions.

HYBRID GRAPE VARIETIES

The following list begins with 19th century American hybrids that many viticulturists classify as native grapes. The French hybrids, often called French American hybrids in recognition of a genealogy traced back to Hermann Jaeger and his colleagues, were developed in France. Other hybrids, such as Cayuga and Steuben, have been developed in the United States.

American Hybrids

Elvira Most histories of winemaking in America credit Jacob Rommel of Hermann with developing this cross between *Vitis riparia* and *Vitis labrusca*. According to the local history of Gasconade County, however, Jacob Rommel, Jr., produced this grape in his father's nursery around 1880. In his 1895 work, *American Grape Growing and Wine Making*, George Husmann states that Jacob Rommel's Elvira first bore fruit in 1869.

Husmann lauded the vine for its hardiness to withstand the worst of Missouri winter temperatures, its resistance to disease, its high productivity and its ability to yield fine wine. Husmann described Elvira as "a beautiful greenish-yellow wine, without foxiness and a delicate and full aroma, resembling Riesling."

Missouri Riesling Another pioneering viticulturist in Hermann, Nicholas "Papa" Grein, also crossed a *riparia* seedling, this one known as Taylor, with a *labrusca* variety. The resulting hybrid, Missouri Riesling, resembled its German namesake only in color. About Missouri Riesling, Husmann wrote that it was "said to make an exquisite white wine."

Delaware Some plant historians claim that the Delaware, a chance cross between *labrusca* and *vinifera* parents, was the last native variety found in the wild. Winemakers have used the Delaware in their wines for more than 100 years. Husmann described it as "a nice little grape, sweet and luscious for the table and makes a fine wine." Friedrich Muench, meanwhile, said Delaware "makes our best and most fiery white wine, very like the finest Rhinewine."

George Husmann was a pioneer viticulturist in Hermann. Some of his experimental vines, named Dry Hill Beauty, still bloom in a vineyard near Hermann.

Niagara The Niagara was developed in 1868. Husmann described it as a cross between Concord and Cassady, another American hybrid. In his notes he describes its berry as "large, slightly oblong, semi-transparent, greenish-white, bronzed in sun, adheres well to the bunch, flesh tender, sweet and melting, good flavor, skin tough and bears handling well."

Muench One of T.V. Munson's creations, the Muench grape produces a crisp, dry red wine. This species was used extensively as breeding stock by Munson and by Hermann Jaeger.

Friedrich Muench once said "With the growth of grapes, every nation elevates itself to a higher degree of civilization."

French American Hybrids

Seyval Blanc Produced from grapes developed by Seyve-Villard (1895–1959), Seyval Blanc wine is one of the most popular vineyard varieties east of the Rocky Mountains. Many people regard the Seyval Blanc as the finest French American hybrid.

Vidal Wine made from Vidal grapes often has the luscious, buttery fullness of a Chardonnay more than the crispness of a Seyval. While its first impression often only tickles the olfactory fancy, a lingering finish embeds a well-made Vidal in the memory taste buds. Its use in blends makes Vidal perhaps the most widely planted wine grape in France.

Vignoles This hybrid shows a particular fondness for Missouri's soil and climate. Vignoles vines are winter hardy and the buds are more frost resistant than other varieties since they open later. The small, compact bunches of mature fruit produce an excellent dessert wine.

Rayon d'Or This white-wine grape was one of Albert Seibel's (1844–1936) early hybrids. Through an intermediary, Seibel received seeds of Hermann Jaeger's American hybrids in 1886. With these seeds Seibel did further grape hybrid research in the St. Julien vineyards of Bordeaux.

Villard Noir and **Villard Blanc** This red-wine grape creation of Seyve-Villard, was described by Philip Wagner in *Grapes into Wine* as capable of making a "firm, well-balanced wine."

Chelois Chelois once piqued the hopes of Missouri winemakers to produce a notable red wine. From Kansas City to St. Louis, wine lovers enjoy debating how to pronounce this exotic name. In general, Missourians around St. Louis prefer the pronunciation that rhymes with Illinois.

Chancellor Chancellor is a widely planted grape in Missouri, finding its way into many proprietary blends. Vinted in a nouveau style, the grape yields an appealing red table wine that does not require years of age to soften its inherent acids.

Chambourcin Developed by Joannes Seyve (1900–1966), this red-wine grape ripens late and produces a highly regarded red wine. Though it has been susceptible to infection, it remains a promising variety in Missouri vineyards.

Baco Noir Originally known as Baco 1, this hybrid was one of the first grapes planted on commercial scale in vineyards east of the Rockies after 1933. In Missouri planting of Baco 1 declined as winemakers turned to Chambourcin and Chancellor, varieties that typically require less aging than Baco Noir to soften tannic acids.

American French-American Hybrids

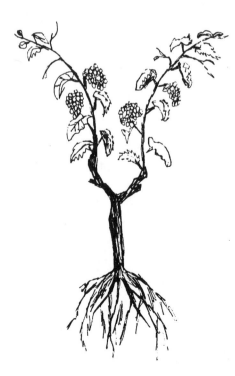

Cayuga White This variety was created at the New York Agricultural Experiment Station in 1972 and is used to produce off-dry wines.

Steuben Developed in New York. The Steuben's lavender grape is most frequently used to blend white wines.

EUROPEAN GRAPE VARIETIES

The following European species, referred to as *Vitis vinifera*, were brought to North America in the 1700s. Until the 1950s they were considered too fragile to be grown suc-cessfully in this climate. Today, however, due to improvements in viticulture, many are thriving in Missouri vineyards.

Chardonnay The white-wine grape of Burgundy, France, Chardonnay contributes its characteristic buttery sensation to the wines of Chablis and Champagne. As much a feeling as a taste, Chardonnay's full butteriness is balanced by an apple-like hardness and crisp acidity. The wine is commonly aged in small oak barrels, a practice that leaves a spicy trace of charred wood in the bouquet and flavor.

Riesling Also known as Johannisberg Riesling, this grape produces the fruity wine of the Rhine valley. Using the *Spatlese* and *Auslese* technique, Riesling grapes reach intense, honey sweetness due to *Botrytis cinerea*, the "noble rot," a skin fungus that removes water and intensifies sugar and flavor. In Alsace, Rieslings are also vinted, though in a drier style than the typical Rhinewine of Germany.

Cabernet Sauvignon The red-wine grape of Bordeaux, Cabernet Sauvignon makes a full-bodied wine that requires long cellar-aging to soften brash tannin. In a balanced wine, the taste of raspberry or blackberry fruit often shines through, offset by herbal overtones. Oak-aging can lend a cigar-box quality to its bouquet.

Pinot Noir The red-wine grape of northern Burgundy, Pinot Noir also plays a significant role in making champagne. With legions of fans who cheer this grape as the number one red-wine variety in the world, the best vintages are smooth and lightly perfumed. Scents of leather or cherries may rise from its bouquet. With less tannin than Cabernet Sauvignon, Pinot Noir is often called an elegant wine.

GRAPE FACT

Is the cork sinking?

Someday you may not need a corkscrew to open Missouri's finest wines. The 2,000 year-old symbol of quality wine—the cork—could be replaced by the ubiquitous screw cap. (Perhaps even more jarring to our aesthetics, a plastic cork, Cellucork, has enjoyed success out in California.) Why the possible shift? It comes down to money, of course. The world supply of quality cork is dwindling, so prices are rising. A winery may spend 25 cents on a cork, whereas an aluminum cap is half a penny.

Cork trees in Spain, Portugal, Tunisia and Morocco are 20 years old before they offer much quality material—and 50 when they really produce the highest grades of cork used in Missouri.

Vineyard crews across the state use both hand- and machine-picking methods.

GRAPES INTO WINE

An Introduction to the Winemaking Process

Winemaking is a process that involves science, timing and a bit of good luck. Although the basic steps involved are easy to outline, one of the best ways to understand the many steps in winemaking is to visit a local winery. From grape harvest to bottling, many smaller Missouri wineries offer interested individuals a chance to participate in the art of winemaking.

Since the time when the first palatable fermented-grape beverage—the first true wine—was enjoyed, many have strived to perfect the process of making pleasing alcoholic beverages from grapes. Today, high-tech processes and advances in agriculture have increased the complexity of a relatively simple fermentation process that has remained virtually unchanged for centuries.

Step 1: The Grape Harvest

Grapes are harvested at the peak of ripeness. One might assume that gauging the ripeness of grapes involves a bit of luck. Although there are many unknowns, vintners obtain an accurate measure of ripeness through the use of a refractometer. A refractometer (read in "degrees Brix") indicates the grape's sugar content, which, as you might of guessed, corresponds to ripeness. Once picked, the harvested grapes are destined to become wine.

Step 2: Crushing

From human feet to high-tech mechanical presses, the result is the same. Grapes are crushed and juice is freed from the skins. It is here that the juice begins to flow.

Step 3: Pressing

Red and white wines take a slightly different course at this stage: Grapes used to produce red wines remain in contact with their skins for several days while those used to create whites are pressed immediately. It is the contact with their skins that yields the robust colors and distinctive tastes of reds. For the pale whites, the juice is immediately gently pressed free of the seeds, skins and stems.

Step 4: Fermentation

Primary Fermentation

The juice or "must" is transferred to containers typically made of stainless steel, oak or concrete. While the majority of wines are produced in large, open containers, premium reds and whites are frequently fermented in small oak barrels to impart an oak taste to the wine.

Yeasts are then added. Feeding on the sugar contained in the skins, these microbes (either natural or synthetic varieties) produce alcohol and carbon dioxide as metabolic by-products. Temperature greatly influences the activity of yeasts, so vintners must pay close attention to this step. Modern refrigeration—like a cool, old wine cellar—allows for uniform and accurate regulation of vat temperature throughout fermentation.

Secondary Fermentation

Production of some white wines involves "malolactic fermentation." This additional step invokes the transformation of malic acid into lactic acid. The second fermentation produces a wine with soft tones.

Fermentation ends when most of the natural sugars have been converted to alcohol. At this point most wines typically have an alcohol content of 7–14 percent. Common labels assigned to wine, such as "dry" or "sweet" are directly linked to the amount of sugar remaining after fermentation has stopped. Dry wines have very little sugar remaining whereas sweet wines have higher sugar contents. Dessert and ice wines are typically the sweetest wines. The term "residual sugar," frequently abbreviated RS, provides a measure of the sugar content that remains in the wine. Typically, the RS value ranges from 1 to 2.5 grams per liter. Dry wines have lower RS values than sweet wines.

Step 5: Aging

At this stage, the wine (both red and white varieties) often appears cloudy and has a rough smell. White wine is commonly aged only a few months and in stainless steel tanks. Premium whites, especially those crafted from Chardonnay and Seyval, may be aged in small oak barrels. When in the confines of oak, whites are often aged "sur lie"—they remain on the yeast sediment.

As for red wines, most endure a much longer aging period. Oak barrels, known as "barriques," are used to store the wine as it matures. Aging in oak barrels is more critical for reds than whites, as the oak serves to combat the tannins that are found in red varieties. These barrels are usually made of either oak from France or white oak from Missouri.

Step 6: Clarification

Sediments are the by-products of fermentation and aging processes. Removal of this unwanted matter is also known as "fining" and can be accomplished by any of a wide variety of methods. Vintners often add beaten egg whites, gelatin or bentonite (a type of clay) to remove the suspended particles from the wine.

Step 7: Filtration

This step adds clarity to the wine and is done just prior to bottling. Many vintners object to clarification and filtering. They argue that vigorous removal of lingering particles robs the wine of important aspects of its character and identity.

Step 8: Addition of Sulfites

Sulfites are added to preserve the wine. A sulfur-based compound such as sulfur dioxide (SO_2)—is a natural by-product of the fermentation process, is commonly used to sterilize and protect wine from spoilage.

Step 9: Aging in the Bottle

Wine is a living product that matures even after the cork is in place. In the bottle, the alcohol, pigments and tannins combine and interact to produce changes in the body of the wine. The growth of a wine in the bottle is continuous (unless the wine has been pasteurized) and time can impart positive or negative effects.

MAKING WINE AT HOME

The nation is affected with grape fever. I firmly believe that this continent is destined to be the greatest wine-producing country in the world. America will, from the Atlantic to the Pacific be one smiling and happy Wineland, where each laborer shall sit under his own vine and none will be too poor to enjoy the purest and most wholesome of all stimulants, good, cheap, native wine.

— George Husmann, 1866

THE GENERAL PROCEDURE

These instructions serve as a basic outline to home winemaking. Some recipes available from your local supplier may call for changes.

1. Get everything ready ahead of time. Double check to make sure all tools and ingredients are at hand. Keep everything that will touch the wine **sterilized**. Sterilize something twice if you think it may be contaminated. Use glass instead of plastic, since air can seep through plastic over time; and use no metals other than stainless steel, since the chemicals in wine can dissolve many other metals.
2. Always dissolve solid **additives** in a little water or juice before adding to must.
3. Add all the ingredients, with the exception of yeast, to the primary **fermenter** and stir until completely dissolved. Don't add all the water if working with a large (5 gallon plus) batch. It is much easier to stir a small amount.
4. Adjust **specific gravity** (S.G.) to about 1.09.
5. Dissolve crushed **Campden tablets** and add to **must**. Let must stand for about a day and then add **yeast.**
6. Ferment until most of the foaming subsides. The rule of thumb says that this should take about a week. At this point the S.G. should be about 1.03.
7. Transfer to a secondary fermentation container, preferably glass. Be sure to carry over a bit of the sediment from the first container. Strain out any fruit solids (if needed). Allow room for foaming. When the foam has run its course (3–24 hr.) top off with cool water or cool wine. Attach the **air lock**.
8. Ferment until the wine clears. You may want to add a **clarifying agent** at the beginning of this stage if the recipe didn't call for it to be added at the beginning. You can also usually wait to add a clarifier even if the recipe called for it at the beginning. Clearing can take three weeks or a few months.
9. Add dissolved Campden tablets (one per gallon) to aging container (glass) then move wine into this container. Top off with cool water and attach air lock.
10. Let set for 2 weeks. If it hasn't produced any more sediment it may be bottled. If you decide to age it, rack it (move the wine off the sediment) every 3 months.

THE HOME WINEMAKER'S DIARY

by Mark Flakne

*All you need to be assured of success in this life
is ignorance and confidence.* —Mark Twain

Day 1: I've taken a big step today, Diary. I visited the local wine and beer supply store to pick out my ingredients and picked the brain of a helpful and knowledgeable clerk. I decided to go with bulk ingredients instead of a kit for two reasons: First, it was cheaper and gave me enough chemicals for another batch; second, I thought I could learn more about making wine if I did it from scratch. When I got home I couldn't wait to get started. I read the recipe on the back of the can of grape concentrate a couple of times and checked my ingredients. When I had my stuff together I chucked it all in the primary fermenter and let the yeast go to work. Then came the hardest part, the waiting.

Here are a few things to remember next time: (1) Everything that comes in contact with the wine should be sterilized, using a method recommended by the supplier or someone else who knows what they're doing. (2) Keep in contact with the supplier. They can be, in any moments of vino-confusion, magically transformed into wine gurus ready to bestow their wisdom—as long as you call between 9 a.m. to 5 p.m. Tuesday through Saturday. (3) Read, read, read . . . you can never know too much—$45 or more is a lot to waste on a botched batch.

Day 7: I buzz home at lunch hour and pop the top off the fermentation bucket, hoping to be overwhelmed with the foam of fermentation. No such luck. The sugary grape sludge is just setting there staring at me with a blank gaze, free of any sign of CO_2.

Day 8: I awake with thoughts of hungry little yeasties grinning from ear to ear as they chow down on the syrupy must of their 5 gallon world. I hop out of bed and run to check my wine. I pull back the top to see what I have been waiting for all this time, small patches of tiny bubbles on the once barren surface. A small but important step in the right direction. Once again I put the lid in place and give the bucket a triumphant swirl (to keep the yeast working).

Day 9: I give the bucket a swirl and hear the happy gurgle of gasses escaping through the clear plastic airlock that sits atop my bucket like some weird hood ornament from the 1960s. After work I hurry home, open the door to the spare bedroom and my eyelids slowly peel back. The walls that were once white are splattered with purple polka dots. The area around the airlock is caked with the remnants of wine foam. I can't resist a peek so I pull back the lid to see my dreams realized—a healthy growth of wispy foam six inches thick. "It's alive! It's alive!" I scream with a wild-eyed grin. My celebration comes to an abrupt halt as my wife plops a wet rag in my hand and stares at the wine-splattered walls not saying a word. "It's alive, it's alive . . ."

Day 10: I construct a makeshift tent from a towel and a coat hanger and fit it over the airlock. The gurgles are steady but I decide to sterilize my mixing spoon (a half-inch dowl rod) and give my concoction a stir. The foam rises, nearing the bucket rim. I put the lid back in place and leave the yeasties to do their thing.

Day 11: The foaming has subsided a bit, but with a brisk stir it comes back to life. It is now time to start thinking about the first racking. I'll wait a few days.

Day 12: I stop by the supply store to pick up some Campden tablets and ask a few questions. The owner says that using wood to stir is not recommended. He tells me that as a rule of thumb I should wait to rack the wine until it has fermented for one week. Needless to say, I purchase a long plastic spoon.

Day 13: Well, Diary . . . I just finished racking my wine. When the first taste of my concoction passed my lips I was elated. It was actually palatable, carbonated and yeasty, but it tasted good to me. The racking went smoothly. I couldn't figure out how to use the valve on the siphon tube so I popped it off and racked it the old-fashioned way, I pinched it off. The foaming took off immediately and this pleased me. Perhaps it will subside tomorrow.

Day 14: After work I return to the supply store to pick up some Sparkolloid clarifying agent so that I will be ready to top off the carboy. When I arrive home I check my wine to see that the foaming has stopped. I add the Sparkolloid according to the directions on the package, top the wine off with cool water and apply the airlock. Now, once again, all there is to do is wait.

Days 15–43: I watch and wait. Slowly my wine begins to clear. I can't wait for my next chance for a taste.

Day 44: Today I racked the wine. I was tempted to try and bottle a bit, but after tasting it I decided that some bulk aging would be in order. It tasted horridly bitter. I think I'll put the carboy in a safe place and forget about it for a while.

Day 74: (A month later) I must bottle now or forget the whole thing. I pop the top on the carboy and siphon the contents into the bottling bucket. I try a sip. Not bad! Not the best wine that has passed my lips but certainly not the worst.

Day 75: Hallelujah! Twenty-five bottles of wine and no place to go. I've died and gone to heaven!

HOMEMADE WINE RECIPES

For the beginner, it's simpler to make homemade wine using juice concentrate than grapes. These recipes make one gallon, but most home winemakers say they come out with better wine when they make a larger batch (just multiply by five). Good luck and happy winemaking!

Blackberry Wine

This is an excellent fruity wine with good body.
Make sure the blackberries are fully ripe and well cleaned before use.

Ingredients
3 lbs. blackberries • 2 ¼ lbs. sugar • 1 gal. water • 1 campden tablet
yeast • yeast nutrient • pectic enzyme • 1 tsp. acid blend

Wash blackberries and place in fermenting vessel. Crush then add a gallon of boiling water. Cool then add pectic enzyme and acid blend and leave for 24 hours. Add the yeast, nutrient and sugar and stir well. Cover and leave for 4–5 days, stirring daily. Pour into a dark fermenting jar and fit a bung and airlock. Wait another 10 days, rack off for the first time. Allow to ferment out and then add the crushed Campden tablet. Clear and bottle.

Strawberry Wine

It is always nice to relax with a light fruity wine on a nice hot day.
Strawberry wine is the perfect wine for such an occasion.

Ingredients
3 lbs. strawberries • 2 ¼ lbs. sugar • ¼ tsp. grape tannin • ½ tsp. citric acid • 1 gal. water • wine yeast • yeast nutrient • pectic enzyme

Use ripe fruit with all bruised flesh removed. Cut up and add to fermenting bin. Add the sugar, citric acid and tannin, then add boiling water. Stir until sugar completely dissolves. Cool, then add the pectic enzyme and stir. Let stand for 24 hours, then add yeast. Put in a warm place to ferment. Stir daily for first five days then rack into a carboy. Fit airlock and bung and return to a warm place. Rack off after fermentation and again after 2 or 3 months. Strawberry wine is best when relatively young, though time maturing smooths the flavor. Be careful to ensure that the wine has fully finished fermenting before bottling, as it is not that uncommon for strawberry wine to begin fermenting in the bottles if corked too early. Makes 6 servings.

THE BASICS OF WINE TASTING

The FIVE STEP Wine-Tasting Method

The basics of wine tasting can be condensed into five simple steps. Keep in mind that the conclusions to be drawn using this method are all relative. What you see, smell and taste in a wine can only have meaning when it is compared to the wines you've tasted before. If you are a beginner, it's time to start building your wine taste index and training your palate by drinking different wines.

SEE

Hold a glass of wine in front of you, against a white background to help you see the finer shade of the wine. You're looking at the clarity and the color of the wine. Look to see how light or dark the wine is; color can be a gauge to its age. Red wines lose color with age whereas whites gain color. When you describe what you see, compare it to something you've seen before (if it's not too obscure).

SPIN

Swirl the wine gently in the glass to release the bouquet. Swirling releases chemicals that combine with air to produce a better smell. The spin also reveals the wine's legs. These are the little streams of wine that run down the glass slowly after the spinning stops. Thicker legs generally mean a higher alcohol content.

SNIFF

Your sense of smell is more sensitive than your sense of taste, so take your time. To train your nose you should try and memorize the smells of some standard wines and let these sensory memories be a guide to experiencing more wines.

SIP

And now for the moment we've all been waiting for, the drink, the sip. Let the wine coat every area of your mouth so that all of your taste buds will have a chance to work. Try and recognize the different flavors and qualities possible in a wine.

SET

Kick back and ponder what you've just tasted. Does it linger pleasantly? Decide whether you like it or not. In the end, drink what you like!

Three More Simple Rules

Although many wine experts suggest enjoying wine through a complicated code of etiquette, only three rules really matter:

1. Hard liquor impairs the taste buds for appreciating the subtleties of wine.
2. Choose the wines you enjoy.
3. Enjoy the wines you choose.

Selecting a Wine

Tradition plays a big part in shaping the rules regarding the pairing of certain wines with different types of foods. Often, cultural biases have further confused the issue. Also, some wine-purists suggest that wine should stand alone and not be considered with food—that food only gets in the way of the wine.

A simplistic view of some of the basic tenants of wine and food pairing could be summed up "red wine with meat and white wine with fish." As useful as this may sound, this generalization is limiting and perhaps, borders on meaningless.

So, how does one match the perfect wine with the food on the table? Today, it has become popular to "drink what you like" and many people now choose wine and food pairings according to their tastes and not a series of rigid rules. But, as good a solution as this might sound, there are pairings that can affect (positively or negatively) the wine or the food.

Some Recommendations:

(The following are not rules—In the end, drink what you like!):

Pair white wines with simple dishes, particularly those that highlight fish and shellfish. The more acidic whites tend to complement these dishes nicely. Try a Riesling with some smoked fish.

Pair red wines, especially those high in tannins, with more complex and deeply textured foods. A natural pairing is a young Norton with a steak.

Pair sweet wines with cheese. A sweet wine will support the rich and salty flavors of many cheeses.

Dry wines and sweet dishes do not make a particularly good match. Sweet dishes should be enjoyed with sweet, full-bodied wines.

Is there a guide for the ordering of wine? Yes, and again, no. The order in which you select different types of wine (with food or alone) can affect the flavors and sensations that you experience. A standard convention is dry before sweet, young before old and ordinary before fine. Again, drink what you like.

Cooking With Wine

In addition to its utility as a savory beverage, wine can also be a particularly useful ingredient. Wine imparts favorable flavors to many foods. When wine is added to hot foods, the alcohol evaporates (along with the calories) while the flavors remain. Wine also acts as a tenderizer and can be added to marinades to improve the texture and taste of many meats.

As a rule—dry white wines tend to complement light and delicate foods like chicken and fish, while red wines are used with beef and heartier fare. Sweet rosé and white wines can be used to supplement the tastes of a wide array of fruit and vegetable dishes. A better rule—DON'T BE AFRAID TO EXPERIMENT. A little wine is unlikely to spoil the flavor of any dish; more likely, you will be pleasantly surprised by its addition.

HOW TO STORE
AND CARE FOR WINE

Store wines in a dark, cool place, either upside down or laying the bottles on their sides. This prevents the cork from drying out, which serves to protect the wine from exposure to oxygen. After opening, store the unused portion in its original bottle, corked, laying on its side, in the refrigerator. Most oak-aged wines will be more flavorful and complex if enjoyed at cool cellar temperature (50° F or warmer), not ice-cold. Wine is very oxygen-sensitive, so use it up as quickly as possible.

If It Tastes Good . . . Drink It!
The case for immediate gratification
by Glenn Bardgett

In the wine world, there seems to be quite a some confusion as to when a wine should be enjoyed. Many people seem to think the older a wine the better it is. Few things in this business, or any other, could be more wrong.

It's been said that the French drink their wines too early because they're afraid the socialist government will confiscate them; that the British drink their wines too late because they admire anything old; and that Americans drink their wines at just the right time because they don't know any better.

The truth is that the proper time to drink a wine is when it tastes best. There is very little in the way of a general rule that can be made. If you judge or predict Missouri wines by looking at other regions of the world, you may be making a big mistake. Certainly some, if not most, of our Nortons can age and compare with the great reds from anywhere in the world. But most other Missouri grape varieties are meant to be purchased, opened and enjoyed in a relatively short time after release.

If the Seyval, Vidal or Vignoles that tasted so great at the winery sits in your hot apartment, or near a sunny window, you may be in for an unpleasant surprise when you finally open it. Yes, storage is important to long-term wine-aging potential, but nearly all our wines taste good when we buy them. Why hang on to them and risk the chance of the wine deteriorating?

People have told me about wines they enjoyed at the winery but were disappointed with when they opened a bottle a year later. I reply, "So, why did you keep it so long? If it tastes good, drink it."

As a lover of Missouri wines, it distresses me to hear complaints from an ill-informed consumer who believes the older the wine is the better it is. My advice: Don't get carried away when you find a wine you like. Buy a six-month supply, drink and enjoy, then go back for more. While you sip your whites, let your Nortons age. Ask the winery about the wine's aging potential, then store the wine in the coolest, darkest, dampest place in your home. My suggestion is always, "Find the place in your home that most resembles Meramec Caverns."

HISTORY OF THE BOTTLE

If you decide to make your own wine you will undoubtedly need to bottle it. The following information, while educational, will also provide you with a load of conversational cannon fodder perfect for any occasion where a bottle is present.

The history of the wine bottle starts with the discovery of silica, or glass as a chemical compound. Today, of course, we know glass exists in nature, as obsidian and rock crystal (quartz) minerals, and is beautiful both in its untouched shape and after craftsmen have used it to create jewelry.

The Roman scholar Pliny the Elder, tells the tale of Phoenician merchants traveling from Syria to Egypt with a cargo of *natron* (sodium carbonate, then used for ceramic pastes and as a cleaning agent). After stopping at the mouth of a river with sandy banks, the merchants unloaded the blocks of natron and cooked dinner. One of them happened to place a hot pot on top of a block. They were later surprised to find that the heat of the fire had melded the sand and *natron* together. *Voilà!* Glass!

Bladder, c.1725

Now it's true that glass is made from a mixture of sand, soda and limestone—but this melting and fusion occurs only at temperatures of 1500°C (2700°F), or greater—far above the boiling temperature achieved by a Phoenician cooking pot. That is to say, you need a furnace designed to obtain and maintain those tremendous temperatures.

The oldest glass furnace was discovered in Egypt in 1891, and dates back to 1370 B.C., during the reign of Amenhotep IV. In this excavation were found numerous glass beads and bottles. The bottles were made using a painstaking method that was substantially unchanged until the first blown glass was produced, more than 1300 years later.

Blown glass began in Syria, around 50 B.C. Perhaps some enterprising glassmaker decided that the solid iron rod used to catch and spin glass threads was unnecessarily heavy and awkward to wield. When the solid rod was replaced with a hollow rod, perhaps the glassmaker blew down the length of the rod to help keep it cooler near his hands. That must have been a keen moment of delight when the molten ball of glass at the other end of the rod suddenly expanded into a bright translucent bubble, glowing and shimmering in the light of the fire. It would be self-evident that when cooled, it would serve admirably as a container for liquids.

Shaft & Globe, c. 1680

Possibilities for new sizes, shapes and forms stretched into the infinity of the imagination. Artisans have focused their creativity on glassware ever since, throughout the world. Colored glass, cut glass, engraved glass, glass with jewels—from the simplest shapes to the most ornate—all have enriched our appreciation for glassmaking.

The Glass Bottle Comes Into Its Own

It wasn't until the 17th century that glassmaking technology advanced to the point that more or less uniform-sized bottles could be consistently produced. At this point, a marriage was possible between the bottle and the cork stopper. The modern international wine trade is a child of this union. When vintners started bottling and corking their wines, they no longer had to ship their product in bulky, awkward clay vessels or wooden barrels. The quality of the wine was not spoiled or changed by its container; in fact, the cork and the glass bottle both benefited the wine in its maturing process.

During the 18th century, wine bottles evolved into the sizes and shapes we recognize today. Made from black glass they became taller and more cylindrical and most assumed the form of today's Burgundy bottle. The first machine to make wine bottles was used in Cognac in 1894, and the age of truly uniform bottle shape and size had begun.

Why So Many Different Shapes?

During the 19th century, wine bottles developed into particular shapes according to the regions from which their contents came. Today, most of the world's great viticulture regions have their own distinctive bottle shapes.

The high-shouldered Bordeaux bottle may have developed its particular shape because older red Bordeaux varietals often have sediment settled at the bottom. When the wine is poured into decanters or glasses, the shoulder helps prevent sediment from escaping with the wine. All red Bordeaux wines, such as Cabernet Sauvignon, Merlot, or Cabernet Franc, are aged in green glass—while all white Bordeaux varietals, such as Sauvignon Blanc or Semillion, are aged in clear glass (with a few exceptions in green).

The elegant, sloping-shouldered Burgundy bottle can also contain either red or white wine. In both France and California, Pinot Noir and Chardonnay are the classic varietals bottled in this shape. Pinot Noir is usually found in green glass whereas Chardonnay may be found in either green or clear glass. In California, Chenin Blanc and Rhone varietals are also usually bottled in this shape.

Onion, c. 1700

Modern Manufacture

Wine bottles are made differently today than they were in Cognac in 1894. Visitors to a major bottle manufacturing plant are struck by the automation of the entire process. One huge facility in California uses eight different machines that can mold over 200 different shapes and produce 1 million bottles a day. Each bottle undergoes extensive testing for clarity, symmetry, uniform neck diameter and strength as it rattles and rolls down the line. Time from the furnace to the shipping carton? A mere one hour and fifteen minutes!

Modern Bordeaux

The furnaces and molds are awesome. A batch of raw materials is tipped into a furnace and fired and mixed for 24 hours before the glass is completely molten and mixed. A combination of gas and electricity is used to maintain a temperature of 2700°C, much higher than the minimal melting point for glass ingredients, but necessary because of the large volume to be melted. The molten glass is dispensed in pre-measured billets and shot into molds directly beneath the furnace. This mold first forms the bottle neck; after 5,000 years this hasn't changed. The rudimentary bottle shape is then lifted into a second mold where it is blown into its final shape. Glowing brilliant orange, it is deposited on a moving belt to begin a process of cooling and testing on its hour-long trip to its shipping container. Perhaps the first Egyptian glassmaker would feel at home in this roaring, flame-lit modern environment and admire a process that remains unchanged in its transforming essence, but revolutionized in its precision and speed.

Modern Burgundy

Compiled from an article in the Simi News
Spring/Summer 1995 Newsletter

GRAPE FACT

The punt of the bottle

Sparkling wine bottles have an indentation at the bottom. For carbonated wines stored under great pressure, it's essential. The depression, or punt, relieves the pressure on the base. Without the punt (or kick, as it is also called) the pressure might blow out the bottom.

For non-carbonated wines, the punt's been there since glass was first blown by hand. A pontil, or wooden stick, was used to secure the bottom of the bottle while the glass blower spun and blew the neck end. Naturally, the stick indented the bottom of the still molten glass. Today, higher quality molded glass bottles do not require the punt, but almost all fine wine bottles retain the punt, more out of tradition than necessity.

WINE COUNTRY MEMENTOS

Preserving Labels

Preserving a favorite wine labels is a great keepsake of a memorable event with friends. To preserve the label, fill the empty bottle with hot water and place it in a bucket of hot water. It usually takes about 3 to 8 hours for the label to peel off.

Take the label out and lay it between two paper towels, followed by a layer of newspaper. Then leave on a counter-top and cover with several heavy books, until it dries.

Creating Corkboards

To make a useful bulletin board, or corkboard, from your explorations, drink a lot of wine, or pester friends and family enough so that they save all their corks for you. Decide how large a board you want for your den, office or kitchen wall . . . and when you think you have enough, use a hot glue gun to glue corks lengthwise to a smooth base surface.

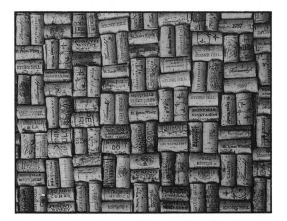

STARTING A VINEYARD

Farmer and artist, drudge and dreamer, hedonist and masochist,
alchemist and accountant—the winegrower is all these things.
— Hugh Johnson *Vintage: The Story of Wine*

Starting a vineyard is one of the most challenging agricultural endeavors one could ever undertake. As one vintner attests, "Starting a vineyard is a lot like eating an elephant. You have to do it one bite at a time." Many vintners will readily tell you that planning, patience and persistence are all essential, along with the much-needed dollar.

Just suppose you read the following steps and begin on the first step tomorrow . . . It could easily take five years before you would be ready to press grapes for wine (assuming the crown gall didn't get you). So what follows is probably just some interesting reading. But if you do have several acres of land and about $5,000 for each acre and a lot of free time, here's your basic outline to an exciting new way of life.

If you lack the land, labor or loan, remember that even a few grapevines can benefit a home's landscape. A few vines not only produce grapes, but provide shade on arbors, trellises and other structures.

Choosing the Land

Missouri grapevines prefer elevated, "frost-free" sites, like bluffs, ridge tops and gently sloped hillsides. Vines on these sorts of sites with good air drainage are less prone to early frosts—which kill emerging flower clusters and reduce potential harvests. The worst places to start a vineyard are small hollows, wooded sites and river bottoms, where frost is more likely to occur. To be profitable in today's market, 30–60 acres are recommended, unless a winery is planned also.

As far as the soil goes, grape vines need a lot of oxygen. Therefore, drainage is important. Healthy vines also need about two feet of unobstructed soil each for healthy root systems.

If a site has all these qualities, its soil should then be tested for its alkalinity or acidity. If tests show a pH outside the range of 5.5. and 6.5, fertilizer or lime should be applied to bring the pH to the recommended level.

Preparing the Site

Preparation is of paramount importance in starting a vineyard. Success comes down to the health of the root systems, which support the vine throughout the life of your vineyard. A diligently tended vineyard can "live" for at least 25 years.

Applying organic matter a year before planting will give young vines a healthy start for several reasons. It will recharge the soil with nutrients necessary to establish a healthy root system. It will also help to offset the cost and labor of introducing fertilizer (which you will have to do eventually).

It will also make the soil easier to work. To reduce the presence of weeds and other plants in a young vineyard, it is important to work the ground over with a plow and disc the fall before cuttings are planted. After the ground has been worked up well, a cover crop like cereal rye or hairy vetch will further reduce weeds.

Ideally, vine rows run north to south to get the most sun. But, if a steep slope precludes this orientation, then east to west will do. Erosion can damage a vineyard much more than less-than-perfect sun exposure. Rows should be planted perpendicular to steep slopes, or along the terraces of rolling hillsides.

Choosing Varieties of Vines

Many Missouri growers are adding French American hybrids and seedless table grapes to their traditional grape varieties. There are dozens of people with good advice on this issue. Whatever you decide, it's best to order vines one or two years before you plant. Also, culls and two-year-old plants don't seem to fare as well as one-year-old dormant-rooted cuttings.

It's also best to diversify your rootstock, since the popularity of specific wines, and therefore demand for a particular grape, continue to change. Consider a grape like Norton, that can be used alone or blended with other varieties, to strengthen your ability to evolve with the industry.

Planting the Vines

When you begin to plant, you will either be planting clippings or one-year-old vines. Clippings arrive with 3 or 4 buds, are about 12 inches long and have no root system. They are dipped in root hormone or "root grow," and then planted directly into rows. When the stems arrive from the nursery, refrigerate them, or plant them immediately if weather permits. Another option is to purchase bare rootstock. Care should be taken to spread the root system as wide as possible.

Use a tractor to cut a furrow to ease planting. Many growers cut a furrow down the row and then plant by hand. Holes should be dug about ten inches deep. Make sure the sides of the hole are not smooth and glazed if using a mechanical auger, since this creates a "pot" effect, which prevents the roots from spreading out. Two vines are usually planted in the same hole, to ensure a keeper. To allow for the best sun exposure, plant the vines six feet apart. Prune the stems down to their two best buds to focus their growing energies. And water each stem well.

GRAPE FACT

A grape is a grape . . .

Even though there is great demand for our grapes, Missouri is not the most profitable place to operate a vineyard. The grapes grown in California's Napa and Sonoma valleys command as much as $2,300 a ton, whereas Missouri's premium red Norton grapes sell for $500 to $1,200, depending mostly on the weather.

To try and fill the demand for Missouri-grown grapes, the state offers financial incentives to grow more. To qualify growers must agree to produce at least three years, with at least a 1.5-ton yield per acre. They must also contract with a processor to buy their fruit. This program is expected to net 39 acres capable of producing on average about five tons of grapes each, enough to make about 250,000 bottles of wine. The state will pay qualified growers about $400 per acre.

Training the Vines

Accounts vary on whether trellises should be installed at planting time, or a year or two down the road. Growers do usually agree about one thing: the trellis should be built to last at least as long as the vineyard. Replacing rotted posts and sagging lines can quickly equal the cost of the initial trellis system.

The point of a trellis is to give the leaves the most sunlight possible, so they can produce hardy plants and high-quality fruit. A standard stretch of trellis has two posts set between 17 and 24 feet apart along a row, with two wires running between them, 2 and 6 feet off the ground.

Sometimes growers use old telephone wire to cut down on costs. If you know someone with a long hedgerow of Osage Orange, you can cut expenses even more by using these native hardwoods rather than buying treated posts.

The importance of a strong trellis system will not become obvious until it's too late to fix it. Many hours of hard-work resupporting existing trellises can be saved each year by starting out with the strongest trellis system you can devise.

Irrigation

Since the quality and depth of soils around Missouri differ greatly, so does the need for irrigation systems. Studies have shown that vineyards in Missouri that use trickle irrigation systems tend to produce a higher-quality and quantity of grapes than those relying on rainfall. Like so many other elements of a vineyard, an irrigation system should be planned out long before the first plant goes in the ground. Most systems are costly. If it's out of your price range, you're not alone—healthy grapes also come from non-irrigated vineyards.

Faurot Hall at SMSU's Fruit Research Station in Mountain Grove.

Advice on the Vine

So you haven't been scared off yet? Well then, fold down the corner of this page for easy reference. For more information, write the Department of Fruit Science at Southwest Missouri State University's Research Campus, Mountain Grove, MO 65711. Or call (417) 926-4105. Fax: (417) 926-6646. Another useful resource is the Department of Agriculture's Grape and Wine Program, P.O. Box 630, Jefferson City, MO 65102. Call (573) 751-6807 or 1 (800) 392-WINE.

Annual Viticulture Field Day

This annual event is held at the State Fruit Experiment Station in Mountain Grove, Missouri. Speakers give presentations on all aspects of commercial grape growing and provide updates on current viticulture research. Tours of the various research plots and facilities are also offered.

Anyone interested in grape growing is welcome to attend. A small fee of $5 will be collected. Call (417) 926-4105 for more information.

The Missouri Winemaking Society

The Missouri Winemaking Society is a group of amateur winemakers who meet monthly to share experiences and to promote wine production. Since the society began in 1977, several members have opened their own commercial wineries. Contact current president Dennis Downing: (314) 355-6575 and past president Greg Stricker: (314) 388-0887, or write: Missouri Winemaking Society, P.O. Box 69331, St. Louis, MO 63169.

EDIBLE LANDSCAPING

Grapevines around a home can offer a precious bit of romantic shade on a hot August afternoon or simply provide fresh fruit for desserts (or wine). Since vines can live 75 years, training them to trellises, arbors and pergolas creates a long-term landscape attraction. If a structure is near the house or where people pass by frequently, most birds will leave the grapes to you.

Trellises

A trellis is a single wire running between two sturdy posts, about 6 feet above the ground. The grapevine's trunk grows straight up to the wire, then two shoots are trained along the wire in opposite directions to make cordons. Fruiting canes arise every 8 inches along the cordons, and shoots drape down on either side forming the curtain. This system is great for the home landscape if you want to make a dense-looking hedge about 6 feet tall or grow the greatest number of varieties in the least amount of space. Yields and sugar levels will be high, and pruning, spraying and picking are easier.

Pergola

A pergola is a series of sturdy poles with exposed rafters. Pergolas have open sides so you can see through them, with the grape foliage overhead, and are usually built to shade patios and walkways. The structure's openness allows breezes to pass through and creates an island of comfort in a hot summer landscape. Each vine should have at least an 8-by-8-foot-square area to cover.

Arbors

When using an arbor, most people plant vines on both sides of an arch-like structure and train them to grow over the arch. The tendency is to prune too lightly, since the idea is to cover the structure with foliage as soon as possible. But light pruning leads to a tangled mass of trunks and canes that then produce poor grapes. Be patient. Prune and train the vines to one trunk and try to leave short fruiting canes, as with a trellis system. To do this, start early on by tying a healthy cane in a vertical direction. Also prune the fruiting canes at intervals of 2 or 3 feet. If these canes are limited to a few buds, the main trunk will become stronger.

A Note on Pruning

Perennial pruning keeps the vines from running wild, which maximizes the potential harvest and improves the fruit quality. Grapes produce fruit only on one-year-old branches, or canes. Without pruning, the fruit-bearing canes spread farther and farther from the trunk. By leaving only the healthiest canes the plant can focus its energy into new growth, and increase the fruit's sugar content.

BIBLIOGRAPHY

Adams, Leon D. *The Wines of America.* 4th edition. St. Louis: McGraw-Hill, 1990.

Bardgett, Glenn. "If It Tastes Good . . . Drink It!" *Missouri Wine Country Journal.* Vol. 7. No. 1. Hermann: Wein Press, spring 1996.

Barnickol, Lynn. "What's In a Barrel?" *Missouri Conservationist*, August 1993.

Borwick, Jim, et al. *Forgotten Missourians Who Made History.* Columbia: Pebble Publishing, 1996.

Burnett, Robyn, and Ken Luebbering. *German Settlement in Missouri.* Columbia: University of Missouri Press, 1996.

Church, Ruth Ellen. *Wines of the Midwest.* Athens: Ohio University Press, 1982.

Denny, James M., Gerald Lee Gilleard and Joetta K. Davis. "Cultural Resources along the Missouri, Kansas and Texas (Katy Trail) Railroad Route, Sedalia to Machens, Missouri." Missouri Department of Natural Resources, Division of Parks, Recreation and Historic Preservation. September 1986 (unpublished).

Denny, James M. "History and Cultural Resources Along the Katy Railroad Corridor: Sedalia to Clinton Section." Missouri Department of Natural Resources, Division of Parks, Recreation and Historic Preservation, November, 1991 (unpublished).

Denny, James M. "Manitou Bluffs Section of the Missouri River." Jamestown: Manitou Publications, 1996.

Dicarlo, Henry, and Chad Finn. "Home Fruit Production: Grape Training Systems" Agricultural Publication G06090. Columbia: University of Missouri–Columbia. October 1993.

Dufur, Brett. *The Complete Katy Trail Guidebook.* Columbia: Pebble Publishing, 1997.

Earngey, Bill. *Missouri Roadsides: The Traveler's Companion.* Columbia: University of Missouri Press, 1995.

Frishman, Robert, and Eileen Frishman. *Enjoy Home Winemaking: A Guide for the Beginner.* 3rd edition. Westport: Crosby and Baker, 1995.

Gabler, James M. *Wine into Words: A History and Bibliography of Wine Books in the English Language.* Baltimore: Bacchus, 1985.

Godley, Lee N., and Patricia O'Rourke. *Daytrip Missouri.* Fulton: Aphelion Publications, 1996.

Holt, Charles. "Weather Fluctuations Have Wreaked Havoc on Grape Production." *Columbia Daily Tribune.* June 17, 1996.

Joseph, Robert. *The Wines of the Americas*. Los Angeles: HP Books, 1990.

Lockshin, Larry. *Establishing a Vineyard in Missouri*. MU Extension Division. Science and Technology Guide.

Meagher, Phyllis. "The Stark Star Shines Again." *Missouri Wine Country Journal*. Vol. 2. No. 1. Hermann: Wein Press, spring 1991.

McMillen, Margot Ford. *A to Z Missouri: The Dictionary of Missouri Place Names*. Columbia: Pebble Publishing, 1996.

Parenteau, Jan. "A-Frame on Bluff Touches Many Lives." *Rocheport Chronicles*. Vol. 2. No. 4. fall 1994.

Pinney, Thomas. *A History of Wine in America: From the Beginnings to Prohibition*. Berkeley: University of California, 1989.

Robinson, Jancis, ed. *The Oxford Companion to Wine*. Oxford: Oxford University Press, 1994.

Scheef, Robert F. *Vintage Missouri: A Guide to Missouri Wineries*. St. Louis: Patrice Press, 1991.

Sichel and Ley. *Which Wine: A Wine Drinker's Buying Guide*. London: Harper and Row, 1975.

Thomas, Marguerite. *Wineries of the Eastern States*. Lee, Massachusetts: Berkshire House Publishers, 1996.

Wagner, Philip. *American Wines and Winemaking*. New York: Alfred Knopf, 1961.

Zraly, Kevin. *Windows on the World: Complete Wine Course*. New York: Sterling, 1997.

WINE COUNTRY ON THE WEB

Interactive Katy Trail: katytrail.showmestate.com
For a biking/hiking adventure in Missouri wine country, the Interactive Katy Trail is a perfect starting point. It lists lodging, services, tips, maps, you name it!

Missouri Wine Country: winecountry.showmestate.com
Inspired by this book, this site includes chat forums, listings of wineries and nearby services, color photographs and numerous tasting and touring tips.

Wine Country of Missouri: www.wine-mo.com
This site is also devoted to Missouri wine country. This great resource contains historical information, lodging, awards and wine country events.

Vino.com: www.vino.com
From St. Louis, this site has tasting descriptions, reviews, a long list of wine links, and even a place to order wine.

WINE GLOSSARY

Acetic: A sharp vinegary odor; Volatile acidity. Too much makes the wine undesirable.

Acid: One of the four descriptive tastes of wine. This taste may sometimes be described as tart or sour and is linked to the areas on the sides of the mouth and tongue.

Air Lock: A loop of hard plastic or glass tubing. When filled 1/3 full of water or sterilizing solution, prevents air from going in while allowing fermentation gasses out. Used to keep bacteria laden air away from the wine while allowing CO_2 to escape.

Arms: Temporary side extensions of the main vine stem—the basal portions of former canes that were left after pruning.

Aroma: The scent of grapes that comes from a wine. Professional tasters make a distinction between aroma and bouquet: young wines have aromas and the more complex qualities of aged wines have bouquets.

Astringent: A rough, puckery taste caused by excess tannin, especially in young wines; diminishes with age in the bottle.

ATF: Federal Bureau of Alcohol, Tobacco and Firearms. This agency oversees the production of wine in the United States.

Aurore: A white French American hybrid grape producing lighter styled soft, fruity wines often finished off dry. Generally produced in the Eastern U.S.

AVA: American Viticultural Area.

Bacchus: Greek god of wine also commonly known as Dionysus.

Baco Noir: A red French-American hybrid grape producing a hearty red wine with some similarities to Cabernet Sauvignon. Generally grown in vineyards in the Eastern U.S. and widely used in Missouri.

Balanced: Having all natural elements in harmony.

Beaujolais (bo-zho-LAY): Fruity and light red Burgundy wine from the region of Beaujolais, France.

Big: Describes a wine full of body and flavor, high degree of alcohol, color and acidity.

Bitter: This is self-descriptive; sign of ill health caused by inferior treatment, i.e., excessive stems during crush or metal contamination.

Bloom: The dusty, whitish covering on a healthy grape on the vine. Helps the grape retain moisture and protects it from spores.

Body: The weight and substance of wine in the mouth; actually a degree of viscosity dependent on percentage of alcohol and sugar content.

Botrytis Cinerea (bow-TRIED-iss sin-eh-RAY-ah): Known as the "noble rot," this mold forms on the grape, making the grape suitable for the production of special types of wine.

Bouquet: How a wine smells to the taster. This term has been used since the 1800s to describe the complex blend of mature wines. Professional tasters often disagree as to when a wine's smell changes from an aroma to a bouquet.

Brilliant: Bright and sparkling; opposite of dull and cloudy.

Brix (bricks): A scale that measures the sugar content in grape juice before fermentation.

Brut (brute): The driest champagne style.

Cabernet Sauvignon (cah-burr-NAY Sow-vee-NYOH): A popular red California varietal. Usually aged for a long time to soften, this wine can produce very complex tastes.

Canes: The mature shoots, those which have become woody after growth has ceased. Fruiting cane merely refers to a one-year-old cane that has the potential to bear fruit.

Carboy: A five-gallon glass container used in the home winemaking process.

Catawba (ka-ta-ba): A *labrusca* grape that is native to America. It is often used in Missouri wines and in wine produced in the eastern U.S. It produces sweet white and blush wines and may also produce dry and sparkling wines.

Cayuga (ki-u-ga): A white American hybrid varietal, producing a light-bodied, fruity, semi-dry wine.

Chablis (shah-BLEE): The northern region of Burgundy, France; any wine made from Chardonnay grapes grown in the Chablis district.

Chambourcin (sham-BOR-sin): This French American hybrid red grape is grown both in the Eastern U.S. and France. It produces fruity red and rosé wines with a distinct aroma. It is an important grape for the Missouri wine industry.

Champagne: This French region produces the only sparkling wine that can truly be called champagne.

Chancellor: A red French-American hybrid known to produce high quality red and rosé wines.

Chaptalization: The process of adding sugar to the juice before fermentation.

Character: The positive and distinctive taste giving definition to a wine.

Chardonnay (shahr-dun-NAY): This wine is the preeminent dry white of California. It is often barrel-aged to produce oak flavors that complement its fruit character.

Chateau (shah-TOH): A house with a vineyard, winemaking facilities and wine-storage facilities on the premises.

Clarity: Wine should have a clear color, should not have cloudiness or visible particles.

Clean: A well-balanced wine with no offensive smell or taste.

Cloying: Too much sweetness and too little acidity.

Color: Wine reflecting proper color of variety; i.e., Vidal Blanc should not be brown.

Common: Adequate, but ordinary.

Concord: A red grape grown widely in Missouri. This grape was partially responsible for the survival of the early Missouri wine industry.

Corky: A disagreeable odor and flat taste of rotten cork.

Crown Gall: A bacterial disease that affects vines. Typically the disease forms fleshy growths on the lower portion of the trunk. Often causes vine death.

Cynthiana (SIN-thee-ana): Thought by some to be the same as Norton, a red American hybrid variety widely used in Missouri. Descriptors of the wine include spice- and coffee-like.

Decanting: A process for separating the wine from its sediments that involves pouring the wine from its bottle into a carafe.

Degorgement (day-gorzh-MOWN): Removal of sediment from the bottle during the making of champagne.

Delaware: A pink-colored American variety used to make sweet, dry and sparkling white wines of high quality when handled correctly. Eastern U.S.

Depth: A rich, lasting flavor.

Dosage (doh-SAHZH): A mixture of cane sugar and wine used in the making of champagne.

Dry: Completely lacking sugar or sweetness; not to be confused with bitter or sour.

Earthy: A peculiar taste that the soil of certain vineyards gives to their wines.

Elegant: Well balanced with finesse and breed.

Enology: The study of wine and the winemaking process.

Estate-bottled: Wine that is produced and bottled by the vineyard owner. Most Missouri wines are estate-bottled.

Fat: Full-bodied but flabby, which in white wines is often due to too much residual sugar—when applied to red wines, means softness and maturity.

Fermentation: The process by which yeast combined with sugar and must produces alcohol; the process of juice becoming wine.

Finesse: Breed and class that distinguish a great wine.

Finish: The taste that wines leave in the end, whether pleasant or unpleasant.

Flabby: Overly soft, almost limp, without structure.

Flat: Dull, unattractive, low in acidity—in sparkling wines; wine that has lost its sparkle.

Flinty: Steely, dry wine, with an odor, and flavor recalling gunflint.

Flor: A kind of yeast produced during some sherry production.

Flowery: A flowerlike bouquet.

Glossary

Foch: A red French American hybrid producing deeply colored wines thought by some to be "Burgundian" in character. This variety is used in Missouri.

Fortified Wine: Wine combined with grape brandy to increase the alcohol content.

Foxy: A pronounced flavor in wines from native American grapes usually in young wines.

Fruity: An aroma and flavor from fresh grapes found usually in young wines.

Full: Full body and color—applied to wines high in alcohol, sugar and extracts.

Gamay (gah-MAY): Red grape used to produce Beaujolais wine.

Green: Harsh and unripe with unbalanced acidity. Causes disagreeable odor and raw taste.

Hard: Tannic without softness or charm; may mellow with age.

Harsh: Excessively hard and astringent; can become softer with age.

Ice wine: A wine made from grapes that have been left on the vine until frozen. The grapes are then harvested and immediately pressed—this porcess yields wine with a higher sugar content.

Insipid: Lacking in character and acidity; dull.

Labrusca: A species of grape native to North America, it belongs to the *Vitis* genus. Concord, Isabella and Catawba grapes are all members of this class. Wine made from this species often has a pronounced flavor described as foxy.

Legs: When a glass of relatively strong wine is tipped just a bit and then set down, the thin streams of wine running slowly back down the inside of the glass to the wine's surface are the legs, or tears.

Light: Usually young, fruity, acidy and with little carbon dioxide.

Long-vatted: Process by which a wine takes on a rich, dark red color by fermenting with the grape skins for a long period of time.

Mellow: Softened with proper age.

Merlot (mehr-LOW): A popular Bordeaux-style red wine similar to Cabernet Sauvignon.

Metallic: An unpleasantly bitter taste from improper treatment.

Must: The pre-fermented grape juice and sugar mixture.

Musty: A disagreeable odor and stale flavor; moldy.

Norton (NOR-ton): A native of Virginia, this grape produces a rich, full-bodied red wine, dry in character which has a unique spiciness.

Nose: Bouquet.

Oxidized: Having lost freshness from air contact, often leaving a sherry-like aroma.

Petite Sirah: A very dark-skinned red grape that produces wines with an inky color. The wine tends to be robust, rustic and simple, often with black pepper in the aroma and taste. This grape is grown successfully in California and Missouri.

Phylloxera (fill-LOCK-she-rah): An aphid, or louse, that destroys vineyards by eating vine roots.

Pinot Noir (PEE-noh NWAHR): This red grape from the Burgundy region of France produces a red wine that is lighter in color than a Cabernet or Merlot. This grape has met limited success in Missouri.

Punt: The concave indentation on the bottom of wine bottles, essential for champagnes, just cosmetic on regular table wines.

Rack: The removal of clear wine from the sediment.

Residual Sugar: Measure of the sweetness of a wine.

Rhineland: English name for the region of Germany known as the Rheinhessen and includes theRheinterrasse. This famous region is dominated by Riesling vines and is admired for its ability to produce some of the finest German wines. (Sometimes used in reference to Missouri's Hermann viticultural area.)

Riesling: A white grape grown in Germany and Missouri.

Ripe: The full-tasting of ripe fruit without a trace of greenness.

Rosé Wines: Wines colored any shade of pink, from barely noticeable to pale red.

Rounded: Well balanced and complete.

Sauvignon Blanc (SOH-veen-yown BLAHNK): This white French grape has declined in use because of the popularity of Chardonnay. This grape produces different flavors when grown in different temperatures.

Seyval Blanc (say-VAL blahnk): This French American hybrid is used all over the eastern U.S. in many different wines. The dry wines coming from this grape are sometimes similar to a French Chablis. This grape grows well in Missouri.

Sharp: Excessive acidity—defect usually found in white wines.

Short: Leaving no flavor in the mouth after initial impact.

Smoky: Descriptive of a bouquet.

Smooth: Of silky texture that leaves no gritty rough sensation on the palate.

Soft: Suggests a mellow wine—usually low in acid and tannin.

Sound: Healthy, well balanced, clean tasting.

Sour: Like vinegar—wines that are spoiled and unfit to drink.

Spice: The definite aroma and flavor of spice from certain grape varieties.

Spurs: These are 1-year-old canes (preferably originating near the trunk) shortened to two buds. Shoots (and later canes) develop from the spur buds. One of these is selected as a fruiting cane for the following season, thus "renewing" the fruiting wood.

Sulphury: A disagreeable odor reminiscent of rotten eggs—if smell does not disappear after pouring wine, this is an indication of a faulty product.

Sweet: High content of residual sugar either from the grapes themselves or from added sugar or arrested fermentation.

Tannic: Sharp, with excessive acidity and tannin; may be necessary in long-lived wines.

Thin: Lacking body and alcohol. Will not improve with age.

Velvety: A mellow red wine with smooth, silky texture leaving no acidity aftertaste.

Vidal Blanc (ve-DAL blahnk): This grape produces a variety of wines including a German-style Riesling—a popular Missouri wine.

Vigorous: Healthy, lively, firm, youthful; opposite of flabby and insipid.

Vignoles (vin-YOLE): A white French-American varietal. This grape possesses complex flavors and aromas, and produces wine ranging from dry to dessert-style wines.

Vinifera: A European species brought to North America in the 1700s. Until the 1950s it was considered too fragile to be grown successfully in this climate. Today many of the most popular grapes grown in Missouri belong to this species.

Vintage: The year or growing season that produced a particular wine; can also refer to the physical process of picking grapes and making wine.

Viticulture: The art and science of growing grapes.

Watery: Thin without body and character.

Weinstrasse: German for wine road (Sometimes used in reference to Missouri's Augusta viticultural area.)

Woody: Odor and flavor of oak due to long storage in barrels.

Yeasty: Smelling of yeast as in fresh bread, often signs of secondary fermentation.

Photo Credits

One hundred and two photographs spanning more than one hundred years of Missouri winemaking history were used to create this book. Many thanks to Jim Anderson and Denise Kottwitz at the Missouri Grape and Wine Program, who allowed extensive reprint permission from their archives. Additional credits go to the owners of Missouri wineries who also generously submitted photographs. Several photographs do appear without credits since many archived images did not include the photographer's names.

R.C. Adams, p. 97, 99, 100–102, 146, 151. Terry Barner, p. 89. Archie Beatte, p. 148. Curtis Bourgeois, p. 81, 84, 86, 87, 88. Lisa Finger, p. 85, 94. Mark Flakne, p. 117. Lucinda Huskey, top p. 68. Randall Hyman, p. 22, 59. Mary Mueller, bottom p. 55. Jane Toben, p. 135. Rick Truax, p. 82. Sue Vanderbilt, p. 1. Michael Vosburg, p. 177. Sandy Watts, top back cover. John Wilding, p. 66. All other photographs by Brett Dufur.

INDEX

A

ADAM PUCHTA WINERY 60
Advice on the Vine 180
American French-American hybrids 160
American hybrids 158
Annual Viticulture Field Day 180
Augusta 34
Augusta Region 25
AUGUSTA WINERY 35

B

Barrel, history of the 128
Berger 72
Best wineries 150
BIAS VINEYARDS & WINERY 73
Biggest wineries 150
BLUMENHOF VINEYARDS & WINERY 31
Boonville, a look back 94
Bottle, history of the 172
Branson 138
BRISTLE RIDGE VINEYARDS & WINERY 100
Budding wineries ripe for exploration 151
BUFFALO CREEK VINEYARDS & WINERY 91
BYNUM WINERY 103

C

Cajun Country 71
Caring for wine 171
CAVERN SPRINGS WINERY 48
Central Region 81
Commerce 147
Commonly asked wine country questions 14
Creating corkboards 175

D

Daniel Boone monument 27

Defiance 42
Deutschheim State Historic Site 57
Dutzow 30

E

Edible landscaping 181

F

FERRIGNO VINEYARDS & WINERY 117
Food and wine 170
French American hybrids 159

G

GLORIA WINERY & VINEYARD 135
Grapes into wine 162

H

HEINRICHSHAUS VINEYARD & WINERY 119
Hermann 54
Hermann Wine Region 53
HERMANNHOF WINERY 63
History of Missouri wine 17
History of the barrel 128
History of the bottle 172
Home winemaker's diary 166
How the A-frame came to "B" 88
How to store and care for wine 171
How to use this book 23
How wine is made 162
Hybrid varieties 158

K

Knob Noster 98

L

LES BOURGEOIS WINERY & VINE-YARDS 84
Licking 129
Lone Jack 102

M

Making wine 162

Making wine at home 165
Marthasville 26
MARTHASVILLE VINEYARDS 28
Missouri vines save European
    vineyards from parasites 20
Missouri's wine industry revival 22
MONTELLE WINERY 37
MOUNT PLEASANT WINE COM-
    PANY 39
Mountain Grove 134
MT. PLEASANT WINERY—ABBEY
    VINEYARD 152

N

Native grape varieties 156
New Haven 76
New World grapes 154

O

Oktoberfest 58
Old world winemaking reaches
    Missouri 19
Ozark Highlands Region 111
Ozark Mountains Region 133

P

PEACEFUL BEND VINEYARDS &
    WINERY 125
PIRTLE'S WESTON VINEYARDS 107
Preserving labels 175
Prohibition—The Dark Years 21

R

REIS WINERY 130
RIVER RIDGE WINERY 148
RÖBLLER VINEYARD & WINERY 77
Rocheport 82
ROSATI WINERY 153

S

SAINTE GENEVIEVE WINERY 144
Southeast Wine Region 141

St. Charles 46
St. James 112
ST. JAMES WINERY 114
Starting a vineyard 176
Ste. Genevieve 142
Steelville 124
STONE HILL WINERY—BRANSON
    139
STONE HILL WINERY—HERMANN
    66
STONE HILL WINERY—NEW
    FLORENCE 152
Storing wine 171
Stover 90
SUGAR CREEK WINERY 43

T

Tasting wine, the basics of 169
Tour tips 12
Touring wine country by bike 13
Touring wine country by boat 13
Touring wine country by car 12
Touring wine country by train 13

V

Vines at home 181
Vineyard, starting a 112
Vintner Profile: Dave Johnson 68
Vitis vinifera varieties 161

W

Welcome to Missouri wine country 23
Western Wine Region 97
Weston 105
Wine country mementos 175
Wine outlets 152
WINERY OF THE LITTLE HILLS 50
Wine recipes 168
Wine tasting, the basics of 169
Winemaking Society of Missouri 180

— The Show Me Missouri Series —

99 Fun Things to Do in Columbia & Boone County
Guide to hidden highlights, galleries, museums, towns, people and history in Columbia, Rocheport, Centralia and Boone County. Most trips are free or under $10. Includes maps and photos. 168 pages. By Pamela Watson. $12.95. ISBN: 0-9646625-2-3

A to Z Missouri—A dictionary-style book of Missouri place name origins
Abo to Zwanzig! Includes history for each town, pronunciations, population, county, post office dates and more. 220 pages. By Margot Ford McMillen. $14.95. ISBN: 0-9646625-4-X

The Complete Katy Trail Guidebook—America's longest Rails-to-Trails Project
The definitive guide to services, towns, people, places and history along Missouri's 200-mile Katy Trail. This third edition covers the cross-state hiking and biking trail from Clinton to St. Charles. Includes maps, 80 photos and more. 168 pages. By Brett Dufur. $14.95. ISBN: 0-9646625-0-7

Daytrip Missouri—The tour guide standard for Missouri
Covers daytrips around the state, including annual events, travel tips, 60 photos and 20 maps. 224 pages. By Lee N. Godley and Patricia Murphy O'Rourke. $14.95. ISBN: 0-9651340-0-8

Exploring Missouri Wine Country
This guidebook to Missouri wine country profiles wineries, including how to get there, their histories, wine tips, home-brew recipes, dictionary of wine terms and more. Also lists nearby bed & breakfasts, services and state parks. 192 pages. By Brett Dufur. $14.95. ISBN: 0-9646625-6-6

Forgotten Missourians Who Made History
A book of short stories and humorous comic-style illustrations of more than 35 Missourians who made a contribution to the state or nation yet are largely forgotten by subsequent generations. Compiled by Jim Borwick and Brett Dufur. $14.95. ISBN: 0-9646625-8-2

River Rat's Guide to Missouri River Folklore and History
A Missouri River classic, documented bend by bend by river rat and historian Cecil Griffith. Throughout his Corps of Engineers career, he compiled tales and history about the river, towns and riverboat calamities. First published in 1974. Reissued with new maps and more. 144 pages. $14.95

The River Revisited—In the Wake of Lewis and Clark
Includes excerpts from the original voyage, as well as modern-day commentary from the 200 years since Lewis and Clark. Includes pull-out map of the Missouri River, 50 photos and journals from a modern-day crew of reenactors. 224 pages. By Brett Dufur. $16.95. ISBN: 0-9646625-9-0

River Valley Companion—A Nature Guide
A nice balance between nature, science and fun. This easy-to-use, illustrated four-season guide identifies commonly seen trees, flowers, birds, animals, insects, rocks, fossils, clouds, reptiles, footprints and more. Features the Missouri River valley's most outstanding sites and nature daytrips. 176 pages. Compiled by Brian Beatte and Brett Dufur. $14.95. ISBN: 0-9646625-1-5

Wit & Wisdom of Missouri's Country Editors
More than 600 pithy sayings from pioneer Missouri papers. Many of these quotes and quips date to the 19th century yet remain timely for today's readers. Richly illustrated and fully indexed to help you find that perfect quote. 168 pages. By William Taft. $14.95. ISBN: 0-9646625-3-1